This book is dedicated to Anita.

Published by
LID Publishing Inc.
524 Broadway, 11th Floor, Suite 08-120,
New York, NY 10012, US

The Record Hall, Studio 204,
16-16a Baldwins Gardens,
London EC1N 7RJ, UK

info@lidpublishing.com
www.lidpublishing.com

A member of:

BPR
Business Publishers Roundtable
www.businesspublishersroundtable.com

Printed in the United States
ISBN: 978-0-9991871-3-5

Cover design: Caroline Li
Layout: Matthew Renaudin

LISA WENTZ

Grace under Pressure

A MASTERCLASS IN PUBLIC SPEAKING

LONDON   NEW YORK   SHANGHAI
MADRID   BARCELONA   BOGOTA
MEXICO CITY MONTERREY   BUENOS AIRES

CONTENTS

INTRODUCTION

"Courage is grace under pressure."
Ernest Hemmingway,
The Old Man and the Sea

Humans are born communicators. From the very beginning of life, we express ourselves with sounds, words, tones, movements and gestures. Consider for a moment the qualities most children have when they first begin to speak. They are honest, authentic, uninhibited and fearless. It's their need to be heard and understood that drives them to communicate. Being liked or agreed with is secondary until parenting and societal influences make children second-guess themselves.

If the tendency to second-guess becomes habitual, we become more inhibited, less confident and more afraid of failure. The stakes become higher at school, at work and in social situations. These feelings are exacerbated when we are faced with speaking to a group of people. Being in front of a live audience is filled with pressure. Not knowing how to cope with this pressure is common. These are not skills we are taught at school or at home. So, the natural physiological response is to become nervous. Distracted by nerves, it becomes difficult to concentrate and we feel less and less graceful.

If you've had a nerve-wracking public speaking experience, you might have begun to think you are simply not good at public speaking and never will be. You may also believe you do not have what it takes to be a great speaker. Or that you are lacking innate qualities that others seem to possess. These conclusions are not based on logic. They are based on an emotional reaction to a feeling of having failed. Let's move on from that feeling by bearing a couple of truths in mind.

The first truth is that everyone at some point has felt like a failure after giving a speech. If that wasn't the case, I would not have written this book. The second truth is that you already possess the core qualities you need to access in front of an audience. These qualities are already a part of who you are. They may have been suppressed or made dormant as you focused on developing other qualities for your career. However, with training, you can access these qualities again and learn how to further develop your public speaking skills.

DEVELOPING SPEAKING SKILLS

In social situations, I'm often asked to provide 'tips' and 'tricks' for public speaking. I find it challenging to do this as I feel it cheapens the work I do. I imagine myself asking a pastry chef for tips and tricks and hearing the response, "Don't burn things." While I believe anyone can benefit from public speaking skills, learning them is not as easy as applying a 'trick'. It requires training. This training is useful for anyone who wants to communicate more effectively.

Developing your speaking skills is a journey. It's a process of developing yourself mentally, emotionally and physically. Through considering what motivates you to speak and how you affect others, you will change the way you think about yourself and your audience. You will also become more familiar with your voice and explore its capacity to share your message and to influence your audience.

Let's look at speakers who are generally considered 'greats'. Great speakers seem like naturals. Chances are, this isn't the case – they may have grown up in environments where eloquent speaking was valued or required, and they may have developed their skills along the way through practice and training. A well-known example is US President Bill Clinton, who began studying and emulating politicians such as John F. Kennedy when he was a teenager. Clinton spoke in public as much as he could in order to gain experience, and as an adult he held at-home podium debates with family members over a period of 20 years to continually refine his public speaking skills. Another example is British Prime Minister Winston Churchill; his ability to captivate audiences was the result of structured, refined writing skills and rigorous rehearsals.

THE THREE AREAS OF TRAINING

This book grew from my desire to bring together the three main areas of a speaker's training. These areas are:
- understanding the obstacles that hold us back
- physical training for vocal power
- applying delivery techniques to enliven performance.

These three areas are rarely addressed in one book, and I do not know of another that gives sufficient attention to their essential importance and interconnectedness.

PART ONE: WHAT HOLDS US BACK

Part One of this book focuses on linking negative experiences in your past with current self-doubt that occurs in meetings, presentations and various arenas of public speaking. This does not mean that everyone who feels a bit nervous when they speak in public has something from their past that they've buried. It is quite normal to feel nervous when you are out of your comfort zone. However, if with practice the nervousness does not decrease, I suggest you look further and see whether something buried from your past is nagging at you.

The self-doubt or nagging feeling might show up purely physiologically. Physiological effects of nervousness include a racing heartbeat, sweaty palms, a dry mouth and many others. What's important here is that you identify *your* precise response to nervousness. By identifying how nervousness affects you on a physiological level, you can begin to lessen its grip on you. Ignoring your responses won't work. They will continue to override your feelings of comfort and ability to stay present in high-stress situations where speaking to an audience – large or small – is required.

By connecting the dots between the past and present and applying the exercises I will provide in this part of the book, you will gain strength in areas you once considered weaknesses.

PART TWO: VOCAL TRAINING

How you use your voice can greatly affect the quality of your experience as a speaker and the experience of your audience. The two key lessons brought forward in this part of the book are to eliminate the habits that are causing strain or interfering with your communication, and to develop full capacities for breath, resonance and articulation.

Training is important and it can help you to develop a stronger presence. Like a fingerprint, we all have our own authentic sound, and our sound may be resonant or restricted, clear or unclear. Your voice is not only the sound you make and the words you speak; it is also your ability to convey a range of emotion with clarity. Lack of tension in your voice will also save your energy. The free flow of resonance invigorates you and engages your audience.

With adequate training, you can learn how to bring more ease and balance to your overall alignment. This will also help to deepen your breathing and free up tension. Through accessing your breath and increasing your lung capacity, you can fuel your voice. This is the basis of resonance and it allows you to add variation and richness to your sound. Finally, this part of the book provides training on articulation, which sharpens and punctuates the quality of your expression.

The exercises provided in this part of the book have been chosen specifically as they are direct and essential practices for supporting a strong vocal foundation. These are not rudimentary exercises. They do, however, enable a clear, step-by-step progression that you can track. You can also adapt these exercises to serve as warm-ups before presentations, or whenever you want to wake up your voice. You will begin to connect with the uniqueness and the power of your voice, and its ability to affect others.

PART THREE: DELIVERY

The goal of this part of the book is to give you reliable techniques to enliven your delivery. These techniques are not altogether new to professional speakers. Some of them have been at the heart of Shakespearean acting training since the early 1900s. I have adapted them throughout my teaching practice to serve as tools for public speakers. If applied correctly, with patience and diligence, they can be used to capture the audience's attention and hold it for as long as needed.

The penultimate chapter of the book, "Presence", takes you through straightforward exercises that bring everything together.

Your stage presence is your ability to reveal authenticity while employing all the principles and techniques that you will have learned. At first, this may involve a lot of conscious effort and practice. In time, however, these delivery tools will become second nature.

MY JOURNEY

I was born in a small college town in Northern California, the youngest of ten children. I had a mother who suffered from histrionic personality disorder and an alcoholic father who suffered from severe post-traumatic stress disorder, having served in but not psychologically survived the Korean War.

Quite a bit of chaos, trauma, neglect and confusion permeated my home. I spent most of my time drawing, fantasizing and trying to tag along with my older brothers. My brothers were attractive, charismatic and extroverted. I saw them as the opposite of myself, and although I had a very large family I was quite often isolated. I was very lucky to be born with an intelligence and a resilience that would later lead me away from my family and into recovering my sense of self.

At the age of 13, I left my home and petitioned the state of California to take me into protective custody. This was an arduous process that took over a year. I went from being an introverted, shy child to speaking to others in a way that made them listen. This was clearly born out of necessity. At that time, I felt as though if I couldn't speak in a way that made people listen to me, I wasn't going to be able to acquire the practical things I needed: a home, school, job and so on.

Fuelled by a deep need to understand my parents' illnesses, myself and others, I vigorously studied psychology throughout high school and college. Looking back, I now realize that this period of my life set the foundation for developing my abilities as an actress, and later as a public speaking coach. At the age of 21 I began studying acting and fell in love with voice and speech training. The process of developing a rich voice that resonated far beyond the back row of a packed theatre was fascinating to me.

Eventually, my love of acting faded and was replaced with a desire to teach and help others find the power in their own voices. I spent several years in teacher-training programs, and I continue to refine my pedagogy today.

MY WORK

Over the past ten years I have coached hundreds of people working to improve their public speaking skills. Many of my clients have shared deeply personal stories with me, and I have shared some of these in this book. I have changed the names, occupations and sometimes locations to protect the individuals' anonymity. I hope you find these stories useful for your development as a speaker.

Part One

What Holds Us Back

The greatest challenges and the greatest opportunities with public speaking are often psychological, stemming from the experiences or conditioning that lie beneath the surface of our daily lives.

In my private practice, I've found that one of my principal roles is to help my clients connect the dots between their past experiences and their ability to develop as public speakers. Once these underlying challenges have been addressed, training as a speaker becomes truly accessible.

Developing a strong speaker's mindset may involve challenging your habitual way of presenting yourself. Many restricting habits are not immediately apparent – or it may be that such habits don't emerge until much later in your process. You may be at an advanced stage of preparing a speech when suddenly you feel a spout of resistance, doubt or anxiety emerge.

This part of the book includes specific exercises that I have developed over the years to address particular patterns or challenges to clear such obstacles and boost confidence.

You may find that some of the material here is not relevant to your needs or to your situation. Feel free to use the information that you feel will support your development. I suggest reading through each chapter first, to see what resonates with you. Then explore the chapters that you feel some resistance to. You might find these exercises illuminate areas not yet explored in your development as a speaker.

1.
Stage Fright

———

Anxiety, Automatic Responses
and Coping Mechanisms

———

"A book may give you excellent suggestions on how best to conduct yourself in the water, but sooner or later you must get wet ... To plunge is the only way."

Dale Carnegie and Berg J. Esenwein,
The Art of Public Speaking

Speaking in public can be a powerful personal experience. It's also a common, often necessary and integral part of being a member of a community. However, it comes with the risk of vulnerability. Essentially, when you stand up to speak, whether on stage in front of hundreds or at a meeting of a dozen people, you have suddenly increased your exposure. You are being seen.

Early humans' experience of being watched closely was intimately interwoven with the very real possibility of a life-threatening event, such as being stalked by an enemy or animal. When speakers say to me, "I hate the feeling of having eyes on me," they are reacting to this feeling of exposure steeped in 500,000 years or more of evolution. It's part of the fight-or-flight response mechanism that we inherited from our ancestors.

This feeling provides the ability to perform the necessary action – take flight, prepare to fight, or freeze. Evolutionarily speaking, we have benefited from this alertness. In modern times, this instinct is naturally triggered when we are in front of an audience – but it is not always so helpful as it was in the past.

In both situations, under an external threat or in front of an audience, we need to work with our physiology. The person in the primal situation needs to gauge their threat and appropriately take action. Doing so increases their chances of survival. The speaker, on the other hand, needs to acknowledge, ground or soothe their feelings, or direct those feelings into their purpose for speaking and their delivery.

THE PHYSIOLOGICAL EXPERIENCE

Most of us, at least once in our lives, have experienced what happens to our bodies when we have stage fright. Your first experience can be surprising. It often appears as soon as you agree to do a speech or when you are first informed that you will be speaking in front of an audience. The simple thought of being in front of others can be that powerful.

On a physiological level, to one degree or another, the fight-or-flight response causes the muscles surrounding the joint connecting your head to your neck to tighten, pulling your head back. When your head is pulled back, your throat muscles tighten and your larynx becomes less flexible. Next, your chest tightens, and you are unable to breathe with the freedom that you are used to. Therefore, less air enters your lungs, your adrenaline level increases and your voice is restricted.

Although there are some speakers who are energized by mild stage fright, most find this experience of mild to severe panic debilitating. Rather than breathing through it and relating to the experience, most follow their primal biology and try to escape it. They look for a way to hide (to get away from the instinctually perceived threat) or they simply try not to feel it (by numbing or suppressing their physiology). When a speaker lacks understanding of why this is happening, they may blame themselves or consider themselves deficient. This kind of negative thinking only increases the challenge.

Essentially, you shouldn't add more fear and self-doubt to compound stage fright. However, this sage advice isn't easy to follow in the moment. Vulnerable situations can trigger all sorts of reactions, defence mechanisms and inner messaging that add to stage fright. To grow and work through this problem, you will need to address what is triggering you.

This is particularly important for a public speaker. An actor builds a character and relies on a script. A dancer has rigorous rehearsals. A singer or musician is typically with others on stage. As a public speaker, you are left to your own devices. You have no one there to catch you if you stumble.

You may want to look to the audience for reassurance. If that reassurance doesn't come, the threat may increase and cause panic. Commonly, the performer can't control the reaction of the audience in any one of these activities. It's similar to a fear of flying. You have no control over whether the plane will crash or not. Yet, if you want to get to your destination, you can't get off the plane. And it is the same with public speaking – you can't walk off the stage.

The key to moving through your primal physiological response is awareness, and the recognition that it is natural. There is no use fighting it – it is better to prepare, accept and work with it. Gradually, rather than perceiving unidentifiable threats that deter you, you can develop a confidence in your ability to be present.

COPING AND HOPING

For those suffering from chronic stage fright, the underlying, compounding causes (the second horse) are often an unrealistic expectation of perfection and a fear of judgment. These mental states make it nearly impossible for speakers to deal directly with their physiology. Instead, they may completely avoid any acknowledgement or preparation in order to keep themselves calm, or start overthinking the event to the point of obsession. Neither of these coping mechanisms works.

Not being prepared only increases anxiety in the long run. By not having done the work ahead of time, you will lack confidence and a clear path to executing your message. There will be a void where the aims and objectives of your talk should be clearly defined and practiced.

After giving a speech you are not fully prepared for, you may say to yourself, "That didn't go as well as it could have, but I wasn't really prepared." So, although there can be a sub-conscious pay-off, the implication is that it's not your fault that the speech didn't go well – rather, the circumstances were to blame. It would be more emotionally risky to prepare a great speech and have it fail. Then the ownership would be completely yours, and it's likely that your inner dialogue would then become very harsh. You tried something new, did your best and failed. You might begin to criticize yourself with thoughts such as "I have no talent" and "I can't do this and I never will be able to." As a result, you might avoid speaking in front of audiences all together. Procrastinating and not preparing give you an escape hatch from a potential downward spiral. However, your presentation inevitably suffers.

In these situations, before speaking, you may experience a period of overthinking and guesswork, which can add to the negative thoughts. A celebrity chef spoke to me about his public appearances and how he felt he was muddling through his talks: "I was speaking way too fast, but I couldn't control it. Afterwards, I realized I left out key points and thought, 'If I could be calmer and talk more slowly it would be so much better.' Yet, with every talk I keep repeating the same mistake over and over." This is a typical comment I hear from clients.

Untrained speakers often compensate for their lack of training by focusing their preparations on drilling their bullet points, and trying to trick themselves into being more relaxed to get through their delivery:

- "I run through exactly what I want to say over and over again in my head."
- "I hear it's good to look over the eyes of everyone."
- "Imagine everyone naked or in their underwear."

Public speaking is a skill. But, without training, you can only guess how it works. Perfectionism and fear of being judged heighten our reactions. Most people tend to overthink, speed up in fear that the audience will lose interest, or forget to breathe. This is about as fruitful as failing to make a soufflé because you didn't consult a recipe and then saying, "I'm not a good cook."

This formula will never be fulfilling.

I'm not suggesting throwing away techniques and tips you've used or invented; rather, I'm asking you to consider that they may not provide a reliable foundation for confidence. In the place where there should be training, most people have an anxiety that is met with ad-libbing, patchwork and guesswork.

ASSESSING THE SITUATION

People experience stage fright in different ways. The extent of your fear may rise or fall depending on the stakes and circumstances of your talk. You may not feel as nervous with a small audience as you do with a large audience – possibly because you perceive the stakes to be lower. Or, you may feel more nervous when you are speaking at a more personal event, such as a wedding, because you perceive the stakes to be higher as you personally know the guests.

It may also be the case that a particular stimulus trips you up – that you are reacting consciously or unconsciously to a certain situation or person. For instance, a client I once worked with had great difficulty speaking before her company's president. The company's president was an authority figure who reminded my client of her father, who had been verbally abusive to her early on in her life. She didn't have any communication training to rely on and simply avoided talking to her president as much as possible, which was having an increasingly negative impact on her ability to do her job. In this situation, my client not only avoided her boss but also avoided the issue altogether in our sessions. Unfortunately, after a few sessions and no significant improvement, she was let go by her employer.

FROM STAGE FRIGHT
TO STAGE PRESENCE

"Have a very good reason for everything you do."
Laurence Olivier

Even the speakers we regard as the greatest have experienced some form of stage fright. After 120 plays and 60 movies, Sir Laurence Olivier admitted that he sometimes experienced such crippling stage fright that he vomited before many opening nights.

The answer to stage fright is not to short-change yourself; it is vital to seek sufficient training to feel prepared and confident. Training prepares you to work on the primal physiological experience of being in front of other people. Training helps you to identify and transform the thoughts that are triggered inside your mind when you feel vulnerable. Training helps you to develop the mindset and skills to work with your instrument – your body and your voice – as well as with an audience, in order to deliver your message.

With training, you can greatly reduce your stage fright, shifting your focus and awareness away from the anxiety you feel. It's like learning to drive a car. Being a passenger doesn't prepare you to drive. Without studying and practising, you may not know how to turn the car on, how to shift gears, how to move the car, let alone smoothly brake or handle turns in icy conditions.

Yet, at some point, you do learn to drive, and you don't need to think about it again. You learn the rules. You integrate the foundations. Now, if something on the road doesn't feel right, you have the tools to work with. It is the same with public speaking. Once you have trained and learned the techniques required to be a confident speaker – physiologically and emotionally – you can rely on your training, your internal guidance and the clarity of your message to help you get through anything on stage.

2.
False Beliefs

—

Compare and Despair,
Impostor Syndrome and
Early Messaging

—

We all carry around beliefs about ourselves, about others and about the world that are not true.

This chapter addresses specific false beliefs that greatly impact the path to confident public speaking. The first is the belief that you should be good at something you haven't trained to be good at. The second is the belief that you are a fraud – that you are not good enough to learn this skill. The third is a potpourri of the negative messaging you may have absorbed in your most formative learning years at home or school.

FALSE BELIEF 1:
COMPARE AND DESPAIR

"There are two types of speakers: those who get nervous and those who are liars."
Mark Twain

The first time I heard the term 'compare and despair' was in the Adult Children of Alcoholics 12-step program. I didn't have to ask what it meant – it was obvious. What wasn't obvious was how much of a trap it is and how many people fall into this trap.

Since I started coaching, I've found that this type of thinking is quite common. I have heard hundreds of clients say:

- "I want to speak like my CEO – she's so natural and eloquent."
- "Public speaking comes so easy to my boss. I want to sound like him, and I don't understand why I don't."

While it may seem natural to compare yourself to others now and again, in this context, it serves no real purpose other than getting you stuck. You begin to think that you are lacking something you cannot have. These kinds of thoughts inevitably lead to a feeling of despair.

A SPEAKER MANIFESTO

What strikes me is that these clients are looking outside themselves for the answers or the direction to becoming a better speaker. But, in fact, the solution is to look internally, at your own mindset, through training. I respond to this type of thinking with a sort of speaker's manifesto:

You are not meant to sound like anyone else. You are meant to sound like you. It's authenticity that audiences crave. A truly charismatic speaker is fearlessly authentic. You need to reveal who you are through the use of verbal language and body language, not through ideals based on comparing yourself to others. The path to becoming a confident speaker is not to become like someone else – it is to discover, develop and bring forward your own physical training, presence and purpose for speaking.

Interestingly, many people who are new to public speaking often wrongly compare their speaking abilities to those of accomplished speakers who have been presenting in front of audiences for many years. There is absolutely no logic to the idea that a first-time speaker should be as eloquent as a speaker who has had years of experience and likely plenty of training.

A similar principle exists in other walks of life. For instance, if you had never played basketball before and decided to go to the park to shoot some hoops, would you think, "Those players in the NBA are so good and natural, why can't I play like that?" Or, if you decided to learn guitar, would you ask yourself after a couple lessons, "How come I'm not as good as Clapton, Townsend or Hendrix?"

You probably wouldn't ask those questions because, for athletes, musicians and many other professions, it's a given that coaching and hard practice are involved. Even the so-called 'gifted' or 'naturals' – the Michael Jordans and the Pavarottis – would not have progressed very far without training and perseverance.

Yet, somehow, when it comes to public speaking, there is this false belief that people are just magically born great speakers.

A PATH TO CONFIDENCE

By considering the paths of great speakers, we can remove false beliefs and learn from their example.

Martin Luther King Jr undoubtedly delivered some of the greatest speeches in US history. During his childhood he regularly attended church, where his father was a reverend. His mother was a musician, who helped train his voice, and on a regular basis he sang in the church choir. In many ways, you could say his speech training was an apprenticeship program through the church and his parents. In high school, he was on the debate team. At 18, he joined the ministry. By the time King was asked to lead the civil rights movement, he had a well-trained voice and years of practice using speech to motivate and inspire his listeners. He was not born a great speaker. He, like many others, evolved into a great speaker through deep desire and rigorous training.

Another example is US President Ronald Reagan – a trained actor who began his career in the early period of Hollywood, when actors were taking daily voice, speech and acting classes. It's no wonder that, by the time he entered politics in the 1960s, Reagan was calm, cool and confident in front of the cameras. His charisma was honed by his drama training, and his practice came through films, serving as president of the Screen Actors Guild and stumping for political causes before his run for the California governorship in 1965. By the 1980s, he was being referred to as the 'great communicator'. But he certainly hadn't been born that way. He had prepared for 40 years.

Another example is Cary Grant. Grant carried a transatlantic accent and a voice with a beautiful melody. A Hungarian client of mine told me that he wanted to sound like Cary Grant in ten sessions – a wish he only shared with me during session eight.

As discussed earlier, comparing yourself to others (especially professional speakers), or expecting to sound like them, will only lead to frustration and possibly despair. You have your own sound and journey to make.

Not even Cary Grant could sound like Cary Grant in ten sessions. It took him many years of practice. If you want to witness a vocal evolution, look at his films from 1932 to 1937. The early films reveal his voice as stiff and choppy. After five years in Hollywood, however, he became the debonair smooth-talker we think of today.

BE INFLUENCED – LEARN FROM THE GREATS

While comparing yourself to others is a quagmire, it can be important and helpful to have role models whose talents, skills and presence inspire you to develop yourself. When you are learning and experimenting, it can even be useful to mimic others and get a sense of what they are doing in order to wake up your own abilities. This is meant to be playful, to inspire your creativity and possibilities, not to replace authenticity. We will go deeper into the subject of learning from other speakers in Part Three: Delivery. For now, here are two simple mindset exercises you can use to develop your craft.

EXERCISE 1

COMPARE AND DELIGHT

Duration: 30 minutes to 1 hour

PURPOSE: SEE SPEAKERS TRANSFORM FROM ROUGH TO POLISHED SPEAKERS

Think of a speaker that you admire.

Select videos of them speaking from 10 or 20 years ago, or early on in their career, and some that are more recent.

Look at the speaker's evolution. Notice their pacing and posture, how they use their eyes, and so forth.

Some excellent examples are Eric Schmidt, former CEO of Google; actress Elizabeth Taylor; and motivational speaker Tony Robbins.

As you look at these and other speakers, think about how they changed over time. You will be hard pressed not to admit that public speaking is a skill — one that can be learned like all skills, whether through direct education, apprenticeships, or self-taught or indirect education such as improvisation classes.

EXERCISE 2
ADMIRE AND APPLAUD
Duration: 30 minutes to 1 hour

PURPOSE: WATCH AND LISTEN TO SPEECHES

You can find hundreds of speeches on TED.com or AmericanRhetoric.com. Some of the speeches you'll find are worth experiencing for their power and beauty, as well as educational value.

Seek out great speeches such as Robert Kennedy's impromptu speech announcing the death of Dr King, Oprah Winfrey's 2018 Golden Globes speech, current speeches by global and national figures, and speeches by local politicians and others in your community.

Bookmark or save speeches you especially admire.

Answer the following questions for each speech:
- What did you notice from the speech?
- What did the speaker do particularly well?
- Which techniques could you implement in your delivery?

HOW TO MEASURE PROGRESS

Typically we measure success by the reaction of others. Did the audience clearly understand your message? Did the audience ask questions you hoped they would ask? These are great questions to ask yourself. However, there is a second layer of measuring progress.

The reality is that even if you deliver the greatest speech in history, you cannot control what your audience will do or what they will think of you. Instead, you need to gauge your progress by the quality of your speaking and your ability to rely on principles and techniques effectively. These are the things you can control. And, as you master them, you will become better able to relate to your audience and convey your message in the most influential way possible.

With this mindset, in order to make progress you need to start where you are, be where you are, and be ready to grow and learn. Establish realistic goals and benchmarks for yourself – both for the quality of your delivery and in terms of welcoming or pursuing opportunities to speak in front of an audience.

Take baby steps and little leaps forward. You may, for instance, have a goal to present at a conference. As you practise the exercises in this book, record yourself and witness tangible shifts in your delivery. If possible, record yourself giving a live presentation and then examine what you did well and what you want to work on in preparation for your next engagement.

Eventually, the goal is to feel confident that you have training – which you've integrated to one degree or another – that you can rely on when you are asked or chosen to present.

FALSE BELIEF 2:
IMPOSTOR SYNDROME

"Impostor Syndrome is a pervasive feeling of self-doubt, insecurity, or fraudulence despite often overwhelming evidence to the contrary. It strikes smart, successful individuals. It often rears its head after an especially notable accomplishment, like admission to a prestigious university, public acclaim, winning an award, or earning a promotion."
Ellen Hendriksen PhD, Center for Anxiety and
Related Disorders, Boston University

Impostor syndrome may float briefly into our lives or it may overtake our inner attitude for several years. As I found out for myself, it may also influence those we associate with in unexpected ways.

Abigail reached out to me via email in June 2012. For ten years, she'd been the creative director of one of the largest museums in the US. She would be launching a series of speaker events starting in September and she wanted to brush up on her speaking skills, as she'd be serving as master of ceremonies.

Abigail showed up for her first appointment at 5pm precisely, well dressed and surprised that my office was small with no waiting room. Seeming to assess my professionalism, her eyes narrowed in on the bleach spots on the sleeve of my grey sweater.

"I was cleaning that mirror this morning and the liquid cleaner left bleach spots," I said. "Looks ridiculous, doesn't it?" Abigail's eyes softened and she nodded. She seemed to forgive me for not being what she expected, and we were free to start.

Abigail was due to present around ten minutes of what I understood to be a much larger presentation. We began with her presenting this material to me. Based on what I saw, I decided to work with her on her posture first, which had a mild kyphosis (upper chest collapsing towards navel), and introduced exercises to reduce a severe vocal fry. She then presented the material again as I recorded. We had increased her vocal resonance enough to hear the possibility of her sound being powerful and authoritative.

It wasn't until the last five minutes of the session, as her voice opened with resonance, that her intense stony expression melted, revealing a warm, friendly smile and eyes full of trust and excitement.

UNDERNEATH THE SURFACE

Our next session started with a full vocal warm-up. Though things were going well, once again Abigail looked stony, and what I perceived to be distrustful. I decided to dig a little deeper by asking her to tell me what she was thinking. She paused for a second and said, "Okay, I'm a fraud. I'm not qualified to be in this position. My fear is that when I'm speaking the audience will be able to see this."

This didn't just surprise me – it shocked me. This was a well-educated, accomplished woman with 20 years of experience in her field, who had rolled out successful programs at one of the largest and most respected galleries in the US.

While most people suffer from self-doubt from time to time, a high achiever with these symptoms experiences self-doubt all the time. They become masters of hiding these feelings, and lead with protectionism and intellectualism.

Abigail would eventually need to more deeply investigate the pervasive feelings she was experiencing and how these shaped many of her actions. Only then could she work on restoring her sense of self-worth.

ANOTHER WAY IS POSSIBLE

"The mind is reluctant to embrace deep change and will play devious games to maintain the status quo."
Kristen Linklater

I have since worked and spoken with others who claimed they had similar issues. Many cope through a sense of resignation. A successful female entrepreneur once said to me, "All high-achieving women have impostor syndrome. You have to just accept it."

I strongly disagree with the idea that impostor syndrome is simply something to be accepted. It is a false belief that perpetuates many attitudes and unhealthy behaviours. It may require effort and support, but to rob yourself of your right to feel valued in any capacity will not only affect you but also directly and indirectly affect others around you. The real challenge is to accept that another way is possible.

EXERCISE 3

CHANGE YOUR MINDSET

*Duration: This will be an ongoing process
that is different for everyone*

**PURPOSE: ACKNOWLEDGE EXISTING UNHELPFUL
THOUGHT PATTERNS AND CREATE NEW,
HEALTHIER PATTERS**

Step 1: The first step in working with impostor syndrome is to acknowledge you are not alone. The experience is very common, even to those who have achieved the highest standards of success in society. Acknowledging your experience serves to break your isolation and the sense of needing to hide. It opens the possibility of sharing with others – whether friends, colleagues or mentors – and finding a new direction.

Step 2: Look for connections. As you acknowledge the feelings and beliefs underlying impostor syndrome, you will likely gain insights into how fears of being perceived as a fraud can drive behaviours from perfectionism to overworking to procrastination. In the case of public speaking, you may be holding back, feeling a great deal is at stake. You may be avoiding personal sharing or avoiding speaking altogether. Explore these connections through speaking with a mentor, counsellor or trusted friend, or through writing.

Step 3: How are you establishing your sense of worth and competency? Is it realistic? Accurate? Helpful? Are you basing it on what others perceive or think? With these types of questions, you gain the power to shift how you define worth and how you show competency.

Step 4: Now consider your accomplishments. Consider your qualifications. Write them down. Read them out loud. Get used to the fact that you have skills, talents, good qualities and qualifications – including the ability to express your strengths and weaknesses. The goal here is not inflated egomania. Rather, by realistically acknowledging your own accomplishments and abilities, you will become better able to acknowledge those of others. In other words, true humility is steeped in a sincere and realistic appreciation of one's own abilities, not fear.

Step 5: The above steps will help you to reset your direction and develop a growth mindset. Moving forward, it is essential to work towards a mindset centred on the process of what you are trying to achieve, rather than the performance or outcome. In the case of public speaking, focus, with a spirit of curiosity, on what you are learning as you cultivate and apply your skills, rather than your performance results. In other words, enjoy the process, not the product. This will open the way to many new discoveries and ways to connect with others.

In addition to the exercise above, there are cognitive–behavioural therapy techniques that have proven extremely successful in changing habits based on self-doubt into more productive attitudes. Whatever path(s) you choose to take, one thing is for certain: impostor syndrome is very common and completely reversible.

FALSE BELIEF 3:
PEOPLE IN POSITIONS OF AUTHORITY ARE ALWAYS RIGHT

"Courage is the power to let go of the familiar"
Raymond Lindquist

It is inevitable that, in today's interconnected and complex societies, we will encounter all sorts of beliefs, ways of teaching and value systems. These will impact and shape us in countless ways. As children, we absorb as much as we can in order to survive, belong, express ourselves, learn and grow. Many of these beliefs and values are nurturing, empowering and stabilizing. However, we also acquire perspectives that restrict and limit our sense of worth, value and direction.

"YOU ARE NOT SMART AND YOU NEVER WILL BE"

Pierre arrived at my office mid-afternoon during the week of Christmas, three days after he first contacted me. At the age of 34, he had been working as the director of operations of a successful Silicon Valley start-up for a year. He was smart, in a happy marriage, had an enviable career and was handsome, personable and fun.

As a Frenchman, he wanted my advice on how to become more fluent in English. As we talked, it quickly became apparent that, although he had traces of a French accent, he was already very fluent in English and his vocabulary and grammar were stellar.

Pierre explained that when he was asked questions that he was unprepared for, he tended to answer without knowing what he wanted to say and overexplained in his answers.

"You see," he said, "I've been worrying about what others think of me for 15 years. Right now, I'm very worried my CEO and others will think I can't retain talent. One of my team members is leaving and another I'm having to let go because he isn't a good fit."

Pierre confided in me about feeling that others would eventually find out he was a fraud. This worry showed up at work and in social situations on a daily basis. He seemed to be emotionally on guard, and wanted to make sure he could handle whatever might hit him at any moment.

From my experience as a coach, I believed this to be a sign of past trauma or from having received severe negative messaging in the past.

I followed up with questions to gauge where his self-worth may have been compromised. Did he receive adequate support and unconditional love from his parents? Yes. Did he have any caregivers that had rejected him in some way? No. What had his educational experience been like?

As it turned out, Pierre had attended a very competitive prep school where he had been under a great deal of stress to achieve and impress. Failure of any kind had not been acceptable. This had clearly been a formative experience in Pierre's life and this feeling of being under too much pressure had stayed with him. However, it did not account for why he'd concluded he was not capable and intelligent.

I asked whether there had been any incidents that had negatively impacted him during this time in his life. Pierre recalled a particular incident without hesitation. "When I was 19, a teacher asked me to explain something in front of the class. After I was done, she said, 'You are not smart and you never will be. Sit down.'"

This had consciously and subconsciously affected Pierre and had shaped the way he saw himself and lived his life, despite the fact he had never before connected the experience to his ongoing worries.

Pierre had internalized and interpreted the abusive comments as "Nothing you do will ever be enough to make up for your lack of intelligence, and you cannot adequately explain anything." In order to keep pretending that he hadn't been harmed by the incident, Pierre kept finding things to label as inadequate, such as his English. He blamed his lack of fluency for his nervousness.

Essentially, the meetings where Pierre's boss asked him questions were mimicking the situation with his teacher all those years ago in the classroom. As an adult, he felt a great deal of anxiety and couldn't answer in a clear and concise manner. This was not due to a lack of intelligence – it was solely due to having spent time in an unhealthy educational environment, where he had received an abundance of negative messaging about his capabilities. As a result, many years later, when he spoke he felt judged.

When these kinds of injustices happen, it can be very difficult to move past them. If they remain buried or unacknowledged, they fester and nag. By bringing this incident into his conscious awareness, Pierre was able to shift his mindset and begin to relate to his anxiety with less judgment.

EDUCATIONAL INSTITUTIONS

"It is the supreme art of the teacher to awaken joy in creative expression and knowledge."
Albert Einstein

Pierre's experience centred on one particular teacher who failed to do her job. Undesirable outcomes are not, however, only the fault of the individual teacher. Educational institutions also may have policies or cultures that undermine a student's self-belief.

I once worked with the CEO of a Silicon Valley non-profit company. Carson was a 36-year-old, highly intelligent and charismatic man. He came to me to work on his public speaking skills for panel discussions, conferences and networking. Running a non-profit means constantly networking to connect with people who may be persuaded to support the organization's work in one way or another.

In our first session, Carson seemed preoccupied with the desire to win people over – to people please in the hope of getting feedback that would confirm his acceptance by others. He internalized missed connections as failure and incompetence on his part. It was clear that his mindset needed to change.

Before attempting to find solutions, I asked whether he knew why he felt the need for acceptance so deeply. He stated, "Oh yes, I grew up in a small town in New Hampshire. It was very racist. Other than my family, there was only one other black family in town. I was called names and bullied throughout my childhood. Even in high school there were racial slurs written on walls in my school. I was always made to feel like I wasn't as good as the other kids."

Although this had affected Carson, it had not kept him from achieving great things. Though he was nervous and shy about introducing himself on panels, after practising owning his accomplishments without apology (Exercise 4) he became a much more confident speaker.

THE WAY FORWARD

As much as you try, there is no way of stopping all negativity and criticism. Whether it's from your teacher, your boss, your co-workers, someone in a position of authority or someone that has influence over your life, you are guaranteed to receive harsh words at some point. What you can do, however, is to learn how to interpret such situations and how to avoid absorbing these messages. You can work on maintaining and cultivating your learning and process-oriented mindset. You can see negativity for what it truly is and understand that it is not a reflection of who you are. Through this attitude, you may find opportunities to skilfully influence your inner attitude. And, overall, you will be building your capacity to be present with others, even with obstacles.

It is important to drill down and identify what you have absorbed throughout your life. How has this affected you, particularly in terms of your communications and public speaking? You may have believed the messages or you may have internalized the judgments. You may not have even known you had the power to challenge what you were being told. However, now you know – and now you have that power. You can take the opportunity to recognize that these messages do not have to be a part of who you are. In doing this, you are directing compassion towards yourself.

The following two exercises are designed to help you let go of old messages that may be stored in your subconscious and to restore any lost sense of efficacy. As you work through them, you may find variations that serve you better.

EXERCISE 4
ACKNOWLEDGE OR ANNOUNCE
THAT YOU WERE WRONGED
Duration: 25–30 minutes

PURPOSE: CREATE YOUR OWN INNER ADVOCATE

STEP 1: WRITE IT OUT

Scan through your educational history year by year and school by school. Write out all the times when you were wronged – even those that happened at home or involved family.

In each case consider:

- What was the exact nature of the incident?
- What part did you play?
- How did you react to or handle the situation in the moment?
- What message or messages did you absorb?
- How did it affect you?

Along with specific incidents, you may discover many influences that shaped your learning and outlook. Don't be surprised if some resistance comes up. You are returning to emotionally charged and unsettling moments. Breaking your thought patterns requires energy and awareness because often your mind will try to convince you that revisiting these incidents equal being victimized. Remember that now, in this moment, you are not a victim. You survived these experiences. You will find renewed power in your voice.

Take your time with this exercise. Being thorough helps to flesh out your full experience. This gives more power to making a conscious choice as to how you wish to move forward at this point in your life.

STEP 2: TALK IT OUT

With a trusted friend, who will not judge you, read what you've written out loud. Having a witness and an ally to support you will help you let go of negative influences. By speaking out loud, you reduce the amount of influence these negative messages have on you. They are no longer fixed or hidden, and no longer occupying the driver's seat of your mind. Speaking out loud, in this sense, is an action that links your inner intention with the outer world. You are claiming your space and affirming your own right to speak.

EXERCISE 5
WRITE YOUR PERSONAL
EDUCATIONAL RESUME
Duration: 20 minutes

**PURPOSE: ASSERT YOUR RIGHT TO
TREAT YOURSELF WITH KINDNESS AND TO
ACKNOWLEDGE YOUR ACCOMPLISHMENTS**

Write your personal educational resume covering pre-school to the present day.

Be specific as to what was happening during your childhood and what experiences you had:
- What did you learn?
- What did you accomplish?

Here's a brief example:
Westmont High School

I was told by my counsellor that I'd never get into Harvard without connections – that I was unrealistic and should settle for a university in my home state. I felt deeply depressed and ashamed for several weeks. I decided that she did not have all the answers and that, with hard work, I could make it happen. I was right. I learned a valuable lesson about staying true to my desires and myself, especially when someone with authority tried to put me down.

Bachelor of Science, University of California

I finished my bachelor's degree while working full time. I was ridiculed in science class by my professor. I had to pretend it didn't bother me. It distracted me from my studies, but I persevered and graduated with a 4.0.

Master's in Business Administration, Harvard University
I finished my master's in an extremely competitive program. Many of my friends were from wealthy families and I often felt that I was not good enough. I resisted talking about my working-class parents. I was often told if I didn't have proper connections, my degree wouldn't matter. I often felt dismissed by my professors. I graduated with honours.

This exercise brings you face to face with your accomplishments and positive qualities. Your mindset is very important here.

Look at your accomplishments and couple them with how you've overcome obstacles. Consider what you are most proud of, or what meant the most to you.

Take your time and work through year by year.

Be as interested in the qualities you displayed – humour, resilience, friendship, etc. – as the goals you reached.

This is not about having perfect results. It's about acknowledging and appreciating your strengths, and how you worked with circumstances. Achievements are often measured by external standards and are not always a reflection of our academic results. For example, you may have dealt with illness, learning challenges, family matters and so on.

3.
The Inner Critic

———

Repetitive Trauma,
Single-Incident Trauma,
Pressure and Neglect

———

*"I am not what happened to me,
I am what I choose to become."*
Commonly attributed to Carl Jung

Your inner dialogues are full of many different voices. These express unique parts of your personality and the messaging you've internalized over the course of your life. Some voices may emerge in your interactions with others, as you play various roles and express yourself in different situations. Other voices may be present in the background guiding your thoughts and actions in ways you may hardly be aware of.

As a public speaker, you need to cultivate an inner dialogue that supports you. This is often easier said than done, however. You may need to bring your attention and efforts to dismantling an inner dialogue that is harsh, judgmental and undermining.

Where does this inner dialogue come from? How does it undermine your efforts? How can you reclaim any damaged sense of power and confidence as you develop as a speaker? This chapter will go further underneath the surface of false beliefs and consider how repetitive trauma, single-incident trauma, pressure and neglect can result in an inner dialogue dominated by a voice that can be called the 'inner critic'.

TRAUMA AND
THE INNER CRITIC

Trauma is often the result of an overwhelming amount of stress that exceeds our ability to cope or to integrate the emotions involved with the experience. Trauma can be indirect, as in witnessing a fatal car crash, or direct, as in being involved in the crash itself. Repetitive trauma, especially in early childhood, has a more severe physiological effect than a single event, as our identity forms around these experiences.

One key difference between average stage fright and the stage fright of a trauma survivor is the presence of a debilitating inner critic. Clients who have suffered repetitive trauma, be it physical, sexual, emotional or a combination, often share their inner dialogues with me. Sometimes these dialogues are so abusive that it would seem impossible to not have a profound effect on how the client relates to public speaking.

THE BRIDGE BETWEEN THERAPY
AND PUBLIC SPEAKING

Therapy, yoga, meditation and many other practices may support people in healing and moving through trauma. But there remains a gap between these modalities and the moment when the trauma actually affects individuals – in this case, when they are speaking in public. You will probably find that your inner critic doesn't show up unless you are in a vulnerable situation or a position that you don't think you can handle. Until you can bridge this gap and work with what arises in the present moment, the strength of your inner critic may continue to undermine you.

The missing link in addressing the impact of trauma on public speaking is talking out loud and physicalizing your inner experience – not imagining it in your head or freezing in one position. Actors know this well. This is one of the reasons for rehearsals. Actors speak the words of their character out loud and explore movements that match the character's words and personality. It is rare for people to do the same for public speaking. It's likely that you hold back the voices and characters influencing your thoughts and movements. However, when you bring these to the fore, you can work very differently, free up energy and make many discoveries.

When I have a client with a strong inner critic, I ask them to say out loud what the inner critic is saying in the moment – that's the moment that needs to be bridged. The physical act of speech itself shows that you have decided to take the upper hand. It defines the inner dialogue, giving it concrete shape and feeling. Then you have the clarity to release your identification with the voice of your inner critic and the disempowering messages it speaks. Those who have worked extensively with their trauma may still need to carry out this step to connect the dots and link their voice to their healing process and maturation as a speaker.

In its secrecy, your inner critic has power over you. With the process of speaking it out, its hold on you shrinks. The power of your inner critic is released and restored to you. You can be present in the room and not be pulled elsewhere – such as into self-doubt and debilitating views.

If you have a strong inner critic, it may be difficult to imagine what it is like not to have one. However, you can take gradual steps towards freeing yourself of this unwanted voice. In a vulnerable situation that seems to require capacities beyond what you have, you will gradually become better able to recognize the false ideas your inner critic is giving you and decide a course of action. You may not suddenly be able to resolve your situation. But you will reduce the amount of negative self-regard and punishing, fearful inner commentary that you experience.

What follows are several client experiences that illustrate how an inner critic develops and how it may show up in a speaker's journey.

IDENTIFYING THE VOICE

"You gain strength, courage, and confidence by every experience in which you really stop to look fear in the face. You are able to say to yourself, 'I have lived through this horror. I can take the next thing that comes along.'"
Eleanor Roosevelt

Betty entered my office for her 6pm appointment 20 minutes late. She looked haggard, out of breath and a bit chaotic. This was our first meeting. Her blue eyes were nearly bloodshot as she sat down, taking a glass of water from my hand. "I need to tell you something," she said in an extremely shaky voice. "I'm terrified."

Betty's eyes filled with tears. I calmly put a box of tissues down in front of her. "You can tell me as much or as little as you would like," I said, hoping she would feel safe and reassured that no matter what she said, I would be able to help her. I also wanted to convey to her that she was perfectly entitled to speak.

"Do you know why you are terrified?" I asked.

"Yes," she answered. "My mother was verbally abusive to me when I was growing up." When I probed for examples, and asked how often, she said, "I was told daily that I was stupid and shouldn't speak ... It lessened as a teenager because I was able to avoid her, but it was still at least once a week."

Though my external demeanour remained calm, internally I was vacillating between sadness and anger. I reassured Betty that she was in a safe place and would not be criticized for being human. We were 15 minutes into the session when I felt I had enough information to discuss solutions.

To reduce her heart rate and the volume of her negative thoughts, and to release some of the tension she was carrying, I taught Betty how to slow down and deepen her breath. She was soon able to focus on her presentation, which related to her work as a researcher. As she delivered her material, every once in a while, she would stop and stare at her laptop. I misinterpreted this as simply thinking through her material.

When she finished, I asked her how she felt: "Did you hear your mother's criticisms while you were presenting?" Betty responded, "Yes, that's why I kept stopping." The problem was that Betty was allowing criticisms from the past to have equal weight with the time she spent talking about her research.

I asked Betty to share the negative messages and in doing so bring them into her conscious mind. From there we used Exercise 6: Say It Out Loud and Exercise 8: A Conversation with Yourself, presented later in this chapter. Verbalizing her negative inner dialogue was painful for Betty, but worth it. I could see that the impact of her inner critic was lessening. A more balanced, less critical inner dialogue began to emerge.

WEARING ARMOUR

Grace entered my office well dressed in a high-collared pant-suit. She was charismatic and well spoken, yet she avoided presentations and public speaking by having her staff present for her at meetings, conferences and panels. She had no issues with one-on-one meetings, but audiences terrified her.

Following a series of questions, she revealed that as a child she'd had a severely deviated septum that had affected her speech. At age 12, she had become self-conscious and her parents had decided it was time for surgery. The surgery had corrected the issue, yet 20 years later Grace still felt too shy and threatened by audiences to present herself publicly.

She made it clear that she had not been teased, bullied or made to feel that something was inherently wrong with her. As we continued our discussion, I assumed that the need for corrective surgery, especially at a young age, had been absorbed in her subconscious mind, leading her to believe that something was fundamentally wrong with her. It was clear this was connected to her debilitating self-consciousness; however, I was not convinced that this alone had caused her fear of public speaking.

I continued to ask probing questions until Grace had a moment of clarity and recounted that she had been sexually assaulted soon after her surgery. She stated that she knew it had affected her in terms of how she presented herself. She always wore high-collared suits, baggy sweaters or blouses. She told me how she felt frightened and began to subtly shake when she felt she was being watched. Grace's response to her assault was to put on armour through her choice of clothing and by distancing herself from audiences.

Grace and I only had one session together. Even though she acknowledged the session hit the areas she needed to address to be comfortable in front of a crowd, she felt the timing was not yet right to start the work.

This kind of story is unfortunately a common one. Survivors of emotional, physical or sexual abuse will often have an inner critic. This critic can have a debilitating effect until the person makes a conscious decision to remove it. If this applies to you, while you might not have had control over what happened at the time your inner critic developed, you do have control over how it affects your choices today.

TOO MUCH PRESSURE

In my professional experience, an inner critic that has developed from unreasonable expectations is one of the hardest to identify. Children who grow up with high expectations to succeed become adept at hiding their inner critic. These clients make excuses for their perceived limitations and fears. They often believe that they were born with these limitations and have to live with them.

Having not been physically abused or verbally assaulted in an obvious manner, it does not occur to them that they have been deeply wronged by their caregivers. Many of these clients were loved and given nice homes and opportunities. However, they were also given strong messaging that failure of any kind was not an option. They were not allowed to have the opportunity to make mistakes and learn from them. Instead, they were pressured to be 'perfect'.

In this environment, children feel an unreasonable amount of responsibility to make their parents or caregivers happy by fulfilling these expectations. Such expectations to succeed at everything are not realistic. Inevitably, children will fail and begin to self-criticize. The physiological responses that result are often the same as those experienced by a person who has experienced trauma more directly. The sensation of being overwhelmed, unable to speak, unable to articulate thoughts clearly or unable to stay present in high-stakes environments becomes normal.

THE ALCOHOLIC OR DYSFUNCTIONAL HOME

Growing up in an environment where your basic emotional and/or physical needs are not secure can send messages similar to the effects of trauma, as described earlier in this chapter. In a home where one or both parents are addicted to a substance, children's needs become secondary and the child will suffer from neglect. In this environment, children begin to question their own self-worth at a young age. From feelings of inadequacy, the inner critic begins to emerge. A child growing up in an environment without adequate love or protection can develop strong undermining thoughts, such as:

- "That was stupid."
- "You will fail."
- "Everyone thinks you are embarrassing."

No matter how hard they try, nothing ever seems good enough.

Some will become perfectionists and justify this voice as one that pushes them to do better and to achieve more; in this way, the perfectionism seems to pay off. However, there is a vast difference between critiquing and criticizing. Critiquing can be a healthy way to develop skills. Criticizing does nothing for you. The inner critic stops you from being able to think creatively about the work you are attempting to articulate. It is a judgmental voice that interferes with your capacity to analyse a situation in a realistic manner.

The inner critic is not to be confused with a realistic critique of your abilities and circumstances. The inner critic is a self-judgment, a force that undermines your self-esteem, self-worth and ability to function. A realistic critique provides you with feedback and gives you a compass on how to develop and move forward. When the inner critic is seen for what it is, and is no longer in charge of your psyche, you will feel you can handle anything.

The exercises that follow will help you to identify and gain power over your inner critic's influence. This is a major challenge because most people will not immediately identify their inner critic as a negative influence. The inner critic becomes something that you are accustomed to or something you identify with. You may also believe it is helpful on some level or that its negative messages reflect the truth in a situation. The truth is, your inner critic only serves to limit you. It needs to be eradicated or transformed as much as possible.

EXERCISES TO REDUCE OR REMOVE YOUR INNER CRITIC

These are the three fundamental steps you can take to reduce the influence of your inner critic. Return to these principles for every exercise in this chapter:

- **Step 1:** Acknowledge that the inner critic exists.
- **Step 2:** Repeat out loud what the inner critic is saying. Declare that these are false beliefs and that you are willing to eradicate them and replace them with facts.
- **Step 3:** Access and enlist a more supportive inner voice to counter the inner critic's influence and to strengthen other aspects of your personality.

EXERCISE 6
SAY IT OUT LOUD
Duration: 10 minutes

**PURPOSE: ACKNOWLEDGE AND
REPLACE SELF-DEFEATING THOUGHTS**

To reduce the power your inner critic has over your thoughts, you'll need to expose it for what it is: abusive, dishonest, inner chatter that serves to undermine your confidence.

Write down a few things your inner critic tells you.

Then, write down the exact opposites to these.

Say them both out loud.

You can do this alone or with a trusted friend or loved one.

Example 1:
- **False belief:** I'm not knowledgeable enough to speak on this subject.
- **Factual replacement:** My resume shows I'm clearly qualified to speak. I am capable.

Example 2:
- **False belief:** I'm an embarrassment at work. My co-workers are judging me.
- **Factual replacement:** My co-workers support me. My boss believes in me, or else they would not have asked me to present my work.

EXERCISE 7

SAY IT OUT LOUD WHILE GIVING A SPEECH

Duration: 10–20 minutes, depending on
how much of your speech you want to cover

PURPOSE: BRING YOUR INNER CRITIC
OUT OF THE SHADOWS

This exercise will help to identify how your inner critic's voice impacts you in the moment – when you are giving a speech. While you may get frustrated when you notice your inner critic, it is only by noticing it that you learn to let go and not react with tension or fear.

Select a speech you are working on, or one you have given in the past.

Deliver this speech as if you were speaking to an audience (or invite a trusted friend, coach or family member to listen to your speech).

Repeat out loud what your inner critic is saying to you in your mind.

Let this rhetoric enter the flow of your speech.

Then return to the speech. If the voice of the inner critic returns, speak it out loud again.

Take your time in the transitions between your critic and your speech. Let there be a pause, or an extra breath, as you maintain your poise.

EXERCISE 8

A CONVERSATION WITH YOURSELF
Duration: 40 minutes

PURPOSE: MINIMIZE OR ELIMINATE YOUR INNER CRITIC ALTOGETHER

This exercise brings various aspects of our psyche into a dialogue. It has its roots in improvisational theatre and in a powerful trauma resolution therapy called 'eye movement desensitization and reprocessing'. Imagine it as a summit or a meeting of the board of directors of your inner life. The purpose is to find, strengthen and activate aspects of your psyche that can counter and replace the influence of the inner critic. Set aside a minimum of 40 minutes to go through it for the first time.

Elements of this exercise mimic public speaking. It involves speaking out loud, simple physical movements, and sharing memories and stories from different viewpoints. We will explore these elements more deeply in Part Three.

STEP 1: PREPARATIONS – THE FOUR PARTS OF YOUR PERSONALITY, FRONT AND BACK

Take a piece of paper and draw a large plus sign in the centre to create four spaces on the page. Each space will be for one aspect (or you might think of it as one voice or personality) within your psyche. Two of these parts are easily seen by others and two are hidden.

The two sections at the top of the page are reserved for your 'front' personalities. These are the sides of yourself that you lead with – the strong parts of who you are that others easily recognize.

The two sections at the bottom of the page are reserved for your 'back' personalities. These are the dominant sides of your personalities that are not easily recognized by others but that nevertheless affect your experience and your decision-making directly. For instance, your inner child is one of your most dominant back personalities. He/she carries a lot of vulnerability and memories from your childhood. If you take the time to explore this side of your personality through this exercise or other means, you will find it is also a source of strength.

Your paper should look something like this.

FRONT **Adult Self**	FRONT **Creative Self**
Inner Critic BACK	**Inner Child** BACK

Some common dominant parts of personalities include:

Adult Self (front personality)

This is the main decision-maker. Goes to work, pays bills, drives kids to school, books vacations. This is the part of your personality that bears responsibility.

Inner Child (back personality)

This is the part of you with the most clarity. This is likely the most centred, grounded and strongest part of who you are. You might dismiss this voice as not useful. This is often the most ignored part of yourself because it also carries your vulnerability. As with any strong part of who you are, listening to it requires practice.

Creative Self (can be front or back)

This is the artistic part of you. It doesn't have to be 'artistic' in the traditional sense. Creativity can be expressed through art, music, cooking and baking, building furniture, gardening and landscaping ... and many other possibilities. This is the part of you that enjoys introspection and indirect connection with others.

Athletic Self (front personality)

This part of you is a part that excels and is rewarded. You may have excelled at sports early in life and changed course, or remained in competitive sports as an adult.

People Pleaser (can be front or back)

Most people have this side to some degree. However, not many have it as a main decision-maker. This is the side of you that habitually compromises your desires. It could be born out of a need to be liked, for example if you were raised by narcissistic caregivers or addicted or abusive caregivers who taught you to put yourself aside for them.

Trauma Self (typically back)

If you have experienced repetitive trauma, you've likely hidden it somewhere deep. In order to get through the trauma, you had to store its effects. Repetitive trauma could have been experienced as a child, teen or adult. Repetitive trauma could be severe physical or sexual abuse, witnessing abuse of others, experiences in war and so on. If you've had these experiences, this is the quiet side of you that doesn't want to engage with others, often feels dissociative (shut down) or is quietly overwhelmed.

Inner Critic (back personality)

This part will likely incite the most physical reaction in you when you hear it. A mild panic might set in and you may have a desire to leave, freeze or disassociate –

or worse, you may listen to this voice as if it's adding value. As stated earlier, there is a difference between critiquing and criticizing. One is healthy, whereas the other aims to hurt your sense of self. The inner critic has no value and needs to be removed.

STEP 2: PREPARATIONS – UNDERSTATING EACH OF YOUR PERSONALITIES

Take a few moments to consider each of the personalities and answer the following questions:

- How old is this personality?
- How do they dress?
- What do they like to do?
- What are the specific needs of this part of who you are?
- How often are these needs met, and is this sufficient?

Then, out loud, in first person (using words such as "I am ..."), introduce yourself by answering these questions. When you are finished, take a moment to let the personality go, then move on to the next personality you identified in Step 1.

When you have covered the first three personalities, go to the section designated to the inner critic personality and ask yourself:

- How old is the critic?
- When did you first notice it?
- What is the critic's main objective or purpose?

STEP 3: DRAWING ON CENTRE STAGE

Go to the centre of a room and create a simple replica of your four-square grid on the floor.

Assign your personalities to specific squares. You are going to have a conversation with these parts. The conversation should take around 30 minutes.

STEP 4: START THE PROCESS
WITH INTRODUCTIONS

Enter each of the first three squares (not the one for the inner critic just yet) one at a time, and enter fully into the attitude and personality of that square. Physicalize it. You are the character – embody it however feels right to you. You'll need to be brutally honest during this exercise and only speak from the specific personality you assign to the square you are standing in.

Then, out loud, in first person ("I am …"), introduce yourself by answering all of the first set of questions from Step 2.

When you are finished, take a moment to let the personality go, then move to the next square.

Lastly, go to the square designated to the inner critic personality and ask yourself all of the second set of questions from Step 2.

The goal is to see each personality as a distinct part of yourself. Each one should be a different age, have a different demeanour, have a different way of dressing, etc. Start by separating them. At the end of the exercise, they will naturally reintegrate except for the inner critic.

You may find drawing pictures of the individual personalities helpful as well as listing their ages and needs or any other information that feels important to you in defining their qualities.

Adult:
Is responsible
and stressed

Creative Self:
Needs time
and solitude

Inner Child:
Needs playfulness

Inner Critic:
Holds group back

STEP 5: THE CONVERSATION

The conversation may begin with a simple question, such as, "Why don't I speak up at meetings?" or "Why do I keep turning down speaking engagements?"

Each personality must provide an answer based on their own perspective, and state what their needs are. Each personality may also comment with their observations on the conversation. When a specific personality is speaking, you must stand in his/her designated square.

When you are in the inner critic's square, you must say out loud what the inner critic says – for example, "I hate this. I don't want to be here." Don't hold back or censor yourself – dig into this personality so you can see and feel it clearly.

After the critic speaks, go to the square of your strongest personality and have this respond to the inner critic and tell the critic to leave.

Note: The strongest personality may vary each time you do this exercise and, of course, as you invite different personalities into the conversation. Often, strength can be found in the inner child or other front personality types. They are the active doers and, often, carry the least hesitation.

STEP 6: AGREEMENTS

During the exercise, each personality will share its needs. The personalities will negotiate to ensure they get time to do what they need in daily life – for example, the Creative Self might ask for an hour a week to play guitar and the Adult Self might agree to find that time.

By the end, you will have made agreements between the personalities that enable you to move forward. Write down the agreements at the end of the exercise to support your recall.

STEP 7: ENDING THE EXERCISE

By the end of this exercise you will feel that your voices and personalities are calmer, and more certain they can regulate your inner critic if it reappears.

As you prepare to shift from this inner stage to the ordinary world, check in with your breath. Take a few slower, deeper breaths as you let go of any characterization. Exit the four squares and take a look around. You are back to the normal room.

COMMENTS ON THE EXERCISE

The power of this exercise is directly proportional to our ability to be truthful and allow these voices to speak. The exercise may bring us face to face with difficult material, thoughts and experiences that are raw. It's important to stay in the process. You are learning to work with yourself in a new way. Gradually this work will enable you to digest your experience and restore choice. With that comes the power to move forward in a new way.

If you have experienced trauma in your life, the intensity and scope of the trauma, and the age when it occurred, may indicate a need to go slower. Be very gentle. Be willing to stop the exercise if you are getting overwhelmed. Breathe. Go to the squares where you get your strength.

If you are hesitating to engage in the exercise, listen for the reasons. You may already hear your inner critic telling you not to do it, or saying it's too stupid, or giving you excuses such as it takes too much time or that it opens you up too much. Tell your inner critic it will get the chance to express itself inside the square. It may feel strange to say things out loud at first. But you are by yourself, so give it a try. You will find it liberating.

You can choose to do this exercise weekly or until you feel the power (or influence) of your inner critic has dropped significantly.

Although I hope that no one reading this book has been the victim of psychological, physical or sexual abuse, the reality is that many readers will have experienced some form of abuse at some point in their life. If you have, there may be a solid reason why your subconscious creates a barrier to enable you to avoid being seen and heard by groups of people. A strong inner critic may be influencing your journey in life and as a speaker. What's important is that you explore and seek to connect the dots. Your awareness will enable you to make clear choices and to cultivate inner voices that truly support you.

4.
Physical Habits And Challenges

———

Unconscious Patterns
and Physical Compensation
after Injury

———

*"It is not the voice that is bad, but the habits
that suppress its freedom."*
Patsy Rodenburg, *Right to Speak*

Throughout life, we integrate many habits and patterns to simply live. Most habits are easy to identify as healthy or unhealthy. Getting adequate sleep is a healthy habit; chain smoking is not healthy. If asked, you could likely list your more obvious daily habits. However, the habits that show up when we speak in front of an audience are typically surprising because public speaking is not something we do daily. The question is – what speaking habits of mind and body do you want to cultivate? And what habits do you want to let go of?

This chapter provides an inventory of various habits, patterns and physical challenges that may impact your public speaking. With that knowledge, you can get your brain to come off autopilot and actively shape the way you interact with the world. You will find the power to choose the habits you wish to have and to identify habits you want to let go of.

UNCONSCIOUS BODY LANGUAGE

Sheila came to me for one session after failing to break into a high-end tech company. After a two-week try-out, the company declined to offer her the job. The only feedback she got was that her communication skills clashed with the company culture. When I first met Sheila, I found her to be smart, funny and qualified, and I was perplexed about why the company hadn't hired her.

It typically takes about 15 minutes of analysis during my first session with a client to determine the biggest obstacle standing in someone's way. With Sheila, however, we were nearing the session's end when the habit finally appeared. I had asked her to describe the company's work environment and her co-workers. As she described her supervisor, she rolled her eyes. While what she said wasn't particularly harsh, her non-verbal communication expressed extreme disapproval.

I asked Sheila whether she was aware of what she was doing with her eyes. She replied with surprise, "Really? No, I didn't know I was doing that. But my father does it all the time. Maybe I got it from him?"

Regardless of where the habit came from, it was clearly deeply ingrained, and almost certainly had shown up on the job. I suggested Sheila work to minimize her 'outer critic' and to investigate why she felt the need to judge others as less competent than herself.

Most of us adopt postural and non-verbal communication habits from the environment we grow up in. Some of these habits are subconscious and some you will be very aware of. You will likely identify with these habits as part of who you are. They are your identity and how you present yourself to the world, and they are connected to your family and home. Although you may take pride in some of these aspects of your identity, you may find that not all of them are helping you to be a better communicator.

Non-verbal communications are very powerful. How you dress, move, gesture and use your eyes are fundamental aspects of how you express yourself and communicate. Training in public speaking involves becoming more conscious of how you are expressing yourself without speaking.

There are as many non-verbal habits as there are people. Observe yourself during casual conversations, meetings and talks. If you can, watch a recording of yourself talking. Do you have any non-verbal habits? What habits have you picked up from your environment, your family and even people you admire? Observe others too – what do you notice about their habits?

Judging your own habits isn't going to help you change them. However, noticing them, getting curious about them and investigating them will help you to get the upper hand. You will start catching yourself in the act and be able to let the habit go. This can feel strangely vulnerable at first. Eventually, you may find something else – an intentional, constructive habit or simply your presence – takes the place of an old habit.

COMMON VOCAL HABITS

Have you ever walked on stage to speak then stopped to clear your throat? Or coughed for no apparent reason? You may not be aware you are coughing, or you may be thinking you are 'clearing your throat' in order for your voice to sound more resonant. The reality is that when you force yourself to cough, you aggravate your voice box and dry out your vocal folds. This decreases the resonance of your voice. The solution is to stop and replace the habit. Try taking a deep breath and then speaking. You'll notice your voice will sound richer and your throat will feel less strained.

Another interesting and common habit is speeding. During a first session with me, about one in seven clients will deliver their speech so quickly that I cannot understand them. If they seem to have a good sense of humour, I say something like, "You speak faster than Usain Bolt runs, and that's not a compliment!" Usually they laugh. If not, I try a more empathetic approach.

If you are someone who speeds through your speeches, ask yourself whether your mindset is causing the speeding. For instance, some clients tell me they are so nervous they just want to get the speech over with as quickly as possible. Others say they think quickly and are afraid of losing their connection to their thoughts if they slow down. Whatever the reason, once you've identified why you speed, you can use the exercises in Chapter 11: Pacing, Pausing and Body Language to help you slow down.

Though it is considered a habit, vocal fry is also a common trait of North American accents, and it is perhaps especially prevalent in California, my home state. It is commonly associated with the 'valley girl' accent. Like most habits, the severity varies from person to person. In my private practice I have noticed women aged 30–45 still carrying this deeply engrained habit, and it can lead to them being perceived as teenagers on the phone or in webinars. This can be very frustrating to a professional with years of experience in their field.

On a technical level, vocal fry is produced by speaking with low breath support. The vocal folds move slower, producing a sound similar to a creaking door slowly opening. Or it might sound like the voice is stuck in the throat. This lack of resonance can lead to an inability to create an emotional connection with the audience, and it can also damage your vocal folds. The exercises in Chapter 7: Resonance are great for tackling vocal fry.

WHEN HABITS LEAD
TO INJURY

When clients come to my studio, I am constantly assessing their voice and how they can improve and support it. There are times when I hear something in their sound that indicates some damage to their vocal tract. Following a comprehensive assessment, if I feel that I cannot bring about a clear change, I will recommend an otolaryngologist – an ear, nose and throat (ENT) doctor – or a speech–language pathologist to diagnose whether there is any damage or injury that needs medical attention.

A voice coach, unlike an ENT, offers more general advice on healthy voice production and capacity by teaching clients to free up their posture, activate breath support, develop resonance, shape sound, and know when their voice is tired and needs rest. The vast majority of people with vocal injuries can benefit in one way or another from this more universal training. In some cases, the cause of a physical condition is long-term misuse of the voice. This can be addressed in voice training by helping to prevent the problem from worsening and by supporting healing.

A client once came to me with a textured sound like Demi Moore. While Moore's sultry rasp has a certain appeal, it is very limiting and hard on her voice. As I assessed the client's vocal use, I came to the conclusion that she might have vocal fold damage. I asked whether she had experienced prolonged periods of dehydration (this dries the vocal folds and causes damage over time). It turned out that she had spent several months working for her company on a project in Africa. She'd become very sick, including severe dehydration, and returned to the US to recover. She told me this was when she'd noticed her voice had changed, but she had never connected her voice's condition to this event.

Other signs that suggest the need for a medical evaluation are difficulty swallowing, a breathy sound, a break in your voice when you change pitch, and pain when speaking.

If you notice any of these conditions, I recommend that you have a medical examination to determine the cause and best remedy. Many conditions are fully treatable, while in other cases you can prevent them from getting worse and limit their impact on your life and your speaking.

HABITS DEVELOPED
FROM COMPENSATION
AFTER SURGERY OR INJURY

Adam came to see me because his voice felt weak and unsupported when he spoke at length to his students in classes. He loved teaching and enjoyed storytelling, and there had been many opportunities that he'd had to give up because of the limitations in his voice. I found that when he spoke, he either pushed his belly out or pulled in and tightened his belly. Basically, he was forcing breath out to fuel his voice. He seemed to have general confusion about how his breath worked with his voice and was relying on force.

In particular, it was interesting that when Adam was not speaking, his breath became smooth, relaxed and supported. The breath coordination was there, but it was not translating to the use of his voice.

It occurred to me that spouts of anxiety or fear when Adam was speaking in public were triggering this reaction. As we explored further, especially the difference between his breathing and speaking pattern, he quickly realized the cause of all of this. Adam had had surgery in his teens – over 20 years ago – on the left side of his belly, which had left him with a large scar. Soon after the scar had healed and he resumed sports and work, he developed back pain and nerve pain in his leg. He managed this over the years with his chiropractor until he started his own bodywork and movement training. This cured him of the back pain as he learned to use his core muscles again. Breath work was a big part of his training and his regular practice. Yet, whenever he used his voice, he tightened his belly or tried not to engage it. To power his voice, he relied on squeezing his stomach muscles, which was tiring and led to a lot of tension around his diaphragm.

We worked to undo these habits and restore a supported breath for Adam's voice using the exercises in Chapter 6: Breath. This was challenging, as using his voice triggered tension from the trauma of surgery. So, I encouraged Adam to find support from even lower in his torso, where he'd not had surgery – from his pelvic floor and back ribs. This helped to integrate the action and give more space and freedom. He started to find more richness in his voice and confidence that he could power his speaking without tension.

Our brains are extraordinary at adapting and finding new ways to do things. Our ability to compensate – even when we develop less desirable habits – is one of our strongest survival tools. We may seek physical therapy to restore strength and functioning after an injury, yet there is often a residue or pattern imbalance left behind. This may show up in myriad ways – how we move, a tendency to feel certain pains and aches, or further injuries. The question here is whether we restore our most efficient functioning when we are able, or whether our compensations become our norm.

Often, while working with clients, I am able to trace a certain specific habit back to an injury or accident earlier in their life. Along with the physical habit, there is often some emotional and psychological energy bound up in the pattern, as if the memory of the accident, illness or surgery is a kind of glue that holds a pattern in place. Undoing these patterns may release these sensations and memories just as the physical tissue releases its immobilizing holds. Gradually, a new habit – a new coordination that is supported by our conscious awareness – becomes familiar.

The habits discussed in this section may or may not apply to you. It's worth investigating whether you have a habit that is not ideal for you and that shows up when you are in the spotlight, speaking in front of an audience or in day-to-day life. No matter what the habit is, it is within your reach to restore conscious choice, strengthen your instrument (yourself) and come from a place of greater freedom. The process of change may involve shifting how you relate to your body, how you centre your awareness in your body and how you relate from there to whatever life throws at you.

Part Two

Vocal
Training

"If you have an opportunity to use your voice, you should use it"
Samuel L. Jackson

Actors refer to their body and voice as their 'instrument' and approach training with the attitude of musicians, learning to tune, to play and to develop capacities.

The path of a speaker, like that of an actor, is to understand and train their vocal use. Before you even walk out to the podium, you should know how your instrument works, and how good use of your instrument impacts the audience and serves your goals.

In this part of the book, I've distilled essential material and exercises to help you integrate physical vocal training into your delivery. The four chapters focus on posture and coordination, breath, resonance and articulation. These are interconnected, and as you proceed in your practice you will bring them all together into one fluid experience.

Keep in mind that your voice is an incredible engineering marvel. Your vocal anatomy is at once extremely complex and ready to sound with no assembly necessary. Many people will go their entire lives giving very little, if any, consideration to how their vocal instrument functions or how to care for it.

To train and harness the powers of your voice, you need to go off autopilot. This involves understanding how sound is produced, eliminating unnecessary tension, and learning to access, enjoy, and rely on your body's natural resonant capacities rather than straining your voice. The best attitude is one of curiosity, experimentation, observation and gradual progress.

In these chapters I share how I work with my clients. As you work your way through the chapters, consider creating your own designated space in which to practise the exercises. If that's not always possible, try to practise wherever you find yourself – a conference room, your office, etc. This will help you to focus and establish a good habit for your pre-speaking routine.

There are exercises that will help you to develop your mindset and attitude. Others are focused on the physical practice. I recommend setting aside 10–20 minutes a day to familiarize and train yourself on these essential skills. You will see the best results if you practise every day.

Once you've integrated the lessons, you can move towards a maintenance routine of several sessions a week. You can also reduce your repetitions and use this routine as a pre-presentation warm-up.

The result of this training is that many public speakers come to enjoy these practices and find they bring relaxation, focus and connection to their daily lives while greatly enlivening their presence on stage.

Later, in Part Three, we will learn how to use the foundations from Part Two in the art of delivery.

5.
Posture And Coordination

The Foundation
of Presence

---

*"Change involves carrying out
an activity against the habit of life."*
Frederick Matthias Alexander

By the time Stephen came to see me, he was regularly losing his voice. He was teaching three courses a week and presenting at conferences around the world, so he was worried that his livelihood and many of his long-sought-after goals were being threatened by this recurring problem. The techniques he had tried – rest, salt gargles, various sprays and warm-up exercises – had not had any long-term impact. He had visited an ear, nose and throat doctor, who had found no permanent damage but had discovered the effects of constant strain on Stephen's vocal folds and recommended he seek my expertise.

People referred to me by doctors usually have very noticeable posture imbalances, which affect the voice considerably. This was not the case with Stephen. At about six feet tall, he stood comfortably upright with his head nicely balanced at the top of his spine. His weight was centred over his hips and feet, and his shoulders were centred, not slumped forward or pulled back as I regularly see in this era of mobile phones and computers. Stephen walked with apparent ease and sat without any unusual struggle or coordination.

I began to cover some introductory questions and continued to observe more closely how Stephen was using his body and voice. Because he was a teacher, he was very comfortable expressing his thoughts in words and he spoke in a relaxed manner. I observed a few minor habits that could easily be resolved, but these were certainly not significant enough to cause the voice loss he was experiencing. To better observe and analyse his vocal use, I asked him to stand by a podium, deliver a few paragraphs of his speech and imagine before him a normal conference audience. His first words told everything! As Stephen began, he threw his head back, disturbing the beautiful balance of his head, neck and spine that I had observed earlier. He arched his back, puffed out his chest, and commenced to push his words and breath out into the space. After hearing a paragraph, I asked him to pause for a moment, to imagine a much larger audience and to be aware that there was no microphone. With these thoughts in mind he resumed. The pattern I had observed, which had been relatively slight before, was now significantly more pronounced.

Next, I asked him whether he knew what he had been doing. Unsurprisingly, he had not noticed. From then on, with the help of his newly found awareness, I coached him on maintaining balance in his body and an awareness of keeping his head on top of his spine. This balance allowed a natural easing of the excess tension in his throat and spine, a more spontaneous ability to breathe with support from his diaphragm and lower torso, and the elimination of the superficial and incomplete upper-chest expansion.

Over five sessions, Stephen was able to establish the new coordination, thus improving his breath support and, in turn, vocal resonance (I will discuss this further in the following chapters). He no longer lost his voice and, most importantly, he was able to present his research with more ease, energy and confidence.

As a postscript, I later learned that Stephen had been a soccer player; this accounted for his grounded, balanced and fluid movements. He had also been a smoker and, although he had quit many years previously, he had carried with him a sense that he could not obtain sufficient air to power his voice. He concluded that this feeling of oxygen deprivation had caused him to compensate and react differently to the stimulus of speaking to an audience; by compensating, he lost the ease of coordination he'd had on the soccer field.

NEUTRAL: POSITION OF POWER AND POISE

This section speaks to establishing or restoring the body's natural posture and increasing your commitment to speaking from this base. By 'neutral posture', I mean being balanced without excess tension or slouching. The knees are hip-width apart, the feet are parallel under the knees and the back has its natural curve without overextension.

Neutral is also a position of power, relationship, connection and poise. It is grounded, balanced, relaxed, aware and dynamic – full of readiness and full of ease.

On the flipside of this high-level posture and coordination, we can and often do lose the coordination and the centred fluency of our movements. This loss can occur because of inactivity or when we hold fixed postures for long periods. Today the habit of sitting all day long while focusing on a screen proves to be a challenging, very dulling and compressing activity for our bodies. We may also lose coordination from cultural conditioning or injuries.

Loss of coordination shows up in two primary ways. Firstly, we lose our innate balance and the beneficial alignment with gravity that we had as children – standing, walking and running with perfect balance and alignment. Secondly, we habitually over use tension when faced with certain ordinary or extraordinary challenges – for example, the loss may appear during an extraordinary experience (such as Stephen's speaking engagements) or during the ordinary act of walking or brushing our teeth. This loss of coordination can show up in every activity we attempt. The impact of this loss of connection is a matter of degree, ranging from various pains to changes in appearance and compromises in our ability to carry out activities or pursue goals.

The impact for a speaker, in particular, is often the development of a strained or limited voice and distracting movements and postural habits. These habits communicate tension to the audience and distract the audience from your content or core message.

The good news in all of this is that we can restore our natural ability, and we can train ourselves to support this in all our activities. The Alexander Technique (discussed next) can help, and I strongly recommend a session to speed up your understanding of this highly kinaesthetic journey of improving posture and coordination.

ALEXANDER TECHNIQUE

Perhaps the most famous system relating to posture and coordination training is the Alexander Technique. Most modern voice exercises are either based on the Alexander Technique or influenced by it. The technique helps us to understand how tension patterns create habits which interfere with optimal posture and how to make the essential changes required to train the voice.

The technique itself was developed out of necessity. Frederick Matthias Alexander was a Shakespearean actor who repeatedly lost his voice. Beginning around 1890, in an attempt to find a cure, he made several discoveries, including what he called the 'primary control of coordination' and how to access it without interference.

The Alexander Technique helps you to restore your mind–body connection by heightening your kinaesthetic sense through the use of touch and improving your ability to meet new stimuli without compromising your equilibrium. It is highly focused on the head balancing on the spine. The opposite of balance in this sense is excess tension.

When the neck is free of tension, the muscles around the voice box relax, allowing for more movement and vocal range.

Similarly, when the chest becomes balanced, the ribcage is able to expand and the lungs can take in more air to fuel speech.

BEATLES AND ROBBINS

The impact of 'good posture' versus 'bad posture' is heightened when we have great performance demands. Sir Paul McCartney is an excellent example of great posture, coordination and vocal use. Take a look and listen to early Beatles footage, and note how free of tension McCartney is. His head balances perfectly on his neck. Today, he has been recording and touring for more than 60 years. In his mid-70ss, his voice is just as beautiful and powerful as it was at age 25.

For an example of excessive tension leading to damaged vocal folds, compare early recordings of motivational speaker Tony Robbins with something he's recorded in the past five years. You will hear a gravelly sound emerge that is due to voice strain, not age!

Robbins is an extremely successful speaker, author and coach. For many years he relied on a high-adrenaline-rush delivery matched by vocal tension. The problem wasn't what he was doing, it was how he was doing it. If he'd been aware, and sought the right kind of vocal training early in his career, he could have achieved just as much, with no damage. This is why training is essential for actors who perform night after night in theatres.

The essential message is to gain awareness of your habits and to restore control over what you are able to control – your own thoughts which stimulate mental and physical patterns.

ASSESSING POSTURE

When a client comes to see me, the first thing I look for is whether they show a visible gravitational downward pull. I call this a 'collapsed posture' because it appears similar to how a marionette puppet drops when its ropes are loose. I observe how this affects the person's breathing and their voice in terms of resonance and breath support. Then I observe how their posture affects their presence and the type of energy they have and are sending out. As an audience member, am I going to watch this person and feel energized or get bored?

One of the most effective things I do is to mimic their posture. Then, I have them stand in front of a mirror and observe themselves. Gently, I guide them out of their collapsed posture and ask them whether they feel different.

After having got their posture free of tension, we tie this posture awareness work into their breath and voice.

POSITION OF POWER

Neutral is the position of power. Standing and walking in neutral – meaning you are not carrying excess tension (or slouching) – is a position of power, whether you are listening, speaking or moving. In neutral you are powerful because you can quickly and easily access your breath, your voice and you can easily perform the actions you need to perform while on stage. In this state, you are authoritative and engaging to your audience.

In contrast, someone with a collapsed posture can potentially bring the energy of the audience in the room down. Speakers rarely consider the audience's experience, whereas in the theatre this is taken seriously. To harness this relationship is the basic goal of method acting (the Stanislavski method of acting). For instance, when a great actor, let's say Dame Helen Mirren, starts to cry in her performance on stage, you might start to cry. It doesn't matter that you are in a theatre with a thousand people. You are intuitively reading and responding to every gesture and sound she makes.

When you have too much physical tension, the chances are that the tension will be extended to the audience. The audience will feel tense as they watch you.

COACHING AND SELF-STUDY

One of the greatest challenges we face is that we get used to our habits – they feel 'right'. We may believe we are standing perfectly upright when we are leaning back. We may also have a certain 'sensory amnesia' where parts of our body are out of our awareness and not active or functioning as they must to give us easeful coordination.

An Alexander Technique teacher can help you recognize when you are interfering with your healthy, balanced posture and help you rebalance and waken your mind–body connection, even in our fast-paced, hyper-stimulated world.

The exercises that follow, nevertheless, can lay a strong foundation and orientation for the work, and will support your presence on stage.

EXERCISES TO ASSIST AND
IMPROVE POSTURE

Posture exercises start with observation. These are mindfulness exercises. You have to tune in to your kinaesthetic sense. This may involve thinking differently about your body and entering your experience in a unique way.

You need to stop thinking that posture refers to a muscular or skeletal change alone. Although changing the way your skeletal system is aligned may lead to a certain freeing of tension in your body, it will not lead to ease of natural coordination.

In these exercises you will first be required to observe yourself and others in an outward sense. Then you will move inward, exploring the concept of getting out of your own way – releasing tension, and letting your coordinating and balancing mechanism function without interference. This may induce shifts in your muscles and bones and, thus, shifts in your overall position and inner experience. From there you can explore the idea of a neutral posture more deeply, and by doing so you will encourage ease and liveliness. Finally, we work with what comes up, with shifting our response to stimuli that cause us to lose our connection or to go into a stress response.

EXERCISE 9

YOUR LIFE IN PICTURES

Duration: 10–20 minutes

PURPOSE: IDENTIFY WHEN AN UNHEALTHY POSTURE BEGAN TO EMERGE

Gather a range of photos of yourself covering your childhood, teenage years and adulthood. Ideally, find pictures in which you are not posing. Note what your posture looked like when you were between two and ten years old, as a pre-teen, as a teen and in your adulthood years.

Does a pattern emerge? At a certain age, you will most likely notice deterioration from your healthy upright posture – where your head is balanced nicely on your neck – to a collapsed or compromised posture to one degree or another.

This exercise will help you to consider the impacts of your experience on your posture and movement. It will also highlight your innate ability to have a natural posture and inspire you to reconnect with it.

EXERCISE 10

GO TO THE MIRROR

Duration: 5 minutes

PURPOSE: ASSESS YOUR CURRENT POSTURE

Stand in front of a full-length mirror with your side towards the mirror.

Stand as you typically stand. Do not change anything.

Notice whether your head is in line with your spine as it was in your childhood.

Notice whether your hips are slightly forward and whether your chest is tilted or sunk inward. Take a photograph and compare it with previous photos.

This exercise demonstrates that your posture is not fixed. It has constantly changed and will constantly change, and we can influence it through what we do. The exercises that follow are designed to increase awareness, release stress and wake up the innate lively functioning of your primary control, which we exuberantly display as young children and lose as we grow into adulthood.

EXERCISE 11
SEMI-SUPINE
Duration: 10–15 minutes

PURPOSE: REDUCE TENSION

This is an essential practice based on F. M. Alexander's work. The semi-supine position (shown below) is very beneficial for developing awareness and releasing tension. When you lie down, you have less desire to be on guard. Your spinal discs rehydrate at rest. Because your entire structure does not need to support itself, any tension is extra tension. You can actively learn to let this tension go. And gravity helps you to do the work.

Lie on the floor or a massage table with a one to two-inch-thick paperback book under your head. (This brings your neck to a natural curve with the rest of your spine – rather than it being overarched.)

Your knees should be up with both your feet flat on the floor, hip-width apart. Let your arms rest lengthwise, bent at the elbow, palms down and resting on your torso.

Stay in this position for ten minutes.

Notice where your torso moves while the lungs fill with air and empty. Your back will begin to lengthen slightly on its own. Your chest will widen and your hips will open up.

Try taking this feeling of length into standing and walking.

EXERCISE 12

OBSERVE THE WORLD

Duration: Ongoing

**PURPOSE: IDENTIFY PHYSICAL
HABITS IN OTHERS**

As you study and develop yourself, you will naturally notice the movements and posture of others. It's easy to find examples of very compromised postures. Focus your attention, instead, on noticing and appreciating graceful, fluid, grounded, well-coordinated movements.

You may find these in abundance in athletes and performers. But you may just as easily find these qualities in a person on the street picking up their bags, a door attendant opening a door, a waiter carrying a tray of drinks or a child running to their parent. Noticing and appreciating these qualities will inspire you and bring energy and value to your own coordination.

In addition, if you travel anywhere in the world where indigenous people still live a life close to nature, take extra time to observe what is unique about their movements and their poise. Explore pictures of people from these regions. With awareness and some training, we can restore our natural poise.

EXERCISE 13
DAILY LIFE – CURIOSITY AND CONNECTION
Duration: Ongoing

PURPOSE: BECOME MORE AWARE
OF YOUR PHYSICAL HABITS

We are creatures of habit – some good, some not so good. We also have a very powerful ability to go on autopilot. This is very important because when the game is on the line, we need full focus on our task. However, if we bring more awareness to noticing our habits during the more mundane moments of daily life, we will find we are able, in the heat of the moment, to release tension and find balance when we most need it.

To begin this exercise, awaken your kinaesthetic curiosity by answering the following questions:
- How are you sitting or standing right now?
- What is the position of your feet? Your head? Your waist?
- Are you breathing?
- Are you balanced?
- Do you notice any unnecessary tension? In your jaw? Your shoulders?

Continue what you are doing while bringing more curiosity and, thus, awareness into the act.

Notice any releases that follow your increasing awareness, and how this may shift your overall position. It's not necessary that you notice any changes in particular.

You may notice that, as you grow more curious and more aware of how you are doing something, you may be less able to actually do it. You may stop altogether for a moment. When this happens, simply let yourself pause a moment before you resume. This is common as we are often more invested in and centred on the action than the means by which we do it.

6.
Breathing

———

Reducing Nerves and
Supporting Your Voice

———

"How do you tell if something's alive?
You check for breathing."
Markus Zusak, *The Book Thief*

James was a business consultant who was responsible for giving several presentations a week. His content preparation was excellent. He had no major issues with posture, and he had a friendly yet authoritative presence. After he delivered his three-minute pitch, I said, "I have just one question – how much were you breathing?" His eyes widened. Smiling like the Cheshire Cat, he replied, "Not at all." With that, he laughed as he realized how silly it was that he had been holding his breath while being completely unaware that he was doing so. The laughter was all he needed to release the tension he was holding on to.

We did a few simple breathing exercises and James presented his pitch again. This time it was fluid, engaging and memorable. It was fascinating to see how releasing one tension pattern (his habit of holding his breath) could make such a drastic difference in his delivery.

Breathing is a very dynamic process. It is automatic – you do not need to think about it for it to happen. Yet, you can bring it under your conscious influence by holding your breath and by activating different parts of your breathing mechanism in different patterns. Even on automatic, your breath is constantly changing due to your changing need for oxygen, your emotional state, your physical position and your overall condition. Breathing is woven into every aspect of our lives and our bodies. Its essential, dynamic and accessible qualities make it a natural medium for meditation, therapeutic intervention and trainings of all kinds.

We can develop breathing habits – conscious and unconscious – that greatly affect our voice. In this chapter, we explore the importance of breathing for a speaker – its mechanics, how to assess your habits, how to change your habits and how to develop your natural capacities.

If you want to be a great speaker, you must learn to breathe like one.

FUEL FOR YOUR VOICE

Breath is produced when the brain sends a message through the phrenic nerve to the lungs and diaphragm. The diaphragm is a lateral sheet-like muscle attached to the ribcage. The diaphragm contracts and moves down, creating negative pressure in the lungs, which allows for natural inhalation or for the air to be pulled in.

During inhalation, the ribcage lifts and widens, expanding the lungs. Air travels into the lungs through the nasal or oral cavity and into the lungs as the diaphragm moves down. The belly feels as though it has increased in size. When we exhale, the diaphragm relaxes, moving upward, which forces air to be expelled from the lungs. The belly and ribcage return to their neutral position.

Tidal breath is the airflow we have during normal breathing patterns in day-to-day use, when we are not taking in a deep breath during exercise, public speaking or singing. This airflow is harmonious and easy. However, in order to produce speech, air flows from the lungs through the vocal folds at a much faster rate. As the high-pressure air speeds through the larynx during exhalation, the process of voiced sound begins. We do not need to do anything to make this process happen. Nature has taken care of that.

The job of a public speaker is to make the powerful breathing fuelling the voice seem as fluid and harmonious as tidal breath. The challenge is to accomplish this without using excess tension. This is the very essence of effective breath work.

Using excess tension, holding your breath or trying to communicate without adequate breath does nothing for you as a speaker.

I cannot overemphasize the benefits of increased capacity and ease of breath – it simply fuels everything else. The resonant sound of your voice, your articulation of sound, your ability to stay focused, your ability to calm an adrenaline rush and your influence on your listeners are all dependent on how you breathe. In addition, your posture and your breath are intimately interdependent.

Freeing your breath frees your posture.

Freeing your posture allows your full breath to happen.

It's relatively easy to improve your breathing, and there is no substitute for practice!

RESTORING GOOD HABITS: AWARENESS FIRST

Most of my clients, easily 90% of them, need some form of breath work. When I first ask them to deliver a speech or presentation, they will hold their breath. This, of course, is not sustainable, as we need oxygen to get to the brain. So, the speaker takes little top-up breaths as they speak. A top-up breath is a short, quick pulling-in of air that lifts the front of the chest and at times it is audible depending on how nervous the speaker is. This is not ideal. We want to hear words, not air. Top-up breaths also decrease the resonant sound of your voice, as they are not enough to support a rich, vibrant sound.

The aim of breathing exercises should be to activate and expand the lower ribs and the back of the ribcage. This is what will give your voice longevity. In other words, breathing fuels your voice so you may speak without the need to quickly pull in tiny bits of air.

LOUDER MEANS BREATH SUPPORT

Many speakers believe, consciously or unconsciously, that they need more tension to speak louder. This is a false belief. In fact, the opposite is true. All you are doing is increasing tension and endangering your voice. You are not increasing your sound.

If you want to regulate how loud you are, train yourself to remain in a balanced, centred posture while activating the muscles already available to you to support vocal power. Your belly needs to remain relaxed and receptive so your diaphragm can drop and your ribs can expand as much as needed to adequately fill your lungs with air. Your support muscles (lower belly muscles, abdominal muscles and pelvic floor muscles) and your diaphragm (which is lifted in order to make you exhale) provide the power for what you want to express. You use them to increase the speed and pressure of the air that vibrates your vocal folds. Think of the sound of your voice as starting with support from the centre of your body, not from your throat.

Change happens when you relearn to rely on your breath the way it naturally functions. Babies are a great inspiration and nature's proof. They cry with an extraordinary lack of tension, excellent activation of their breathing and great loudness for long periods without damage to their voice.

CONSCIOUS BREATHING

With my clients, the first thing I look for is whether they are breathing at all. And, if they are, how are they breathing? Are they using a top-up breath?

When you don't breathe enough or if you are only topping up your breaths, you are just giving yourself the bare minimum of oxygen needed to survive or so that you don't pass out. This kind of breathing is not sustainable for speech.

Think about:
- Is air flowing in and out without a lot of interference?
- Are you arching your back, pulling your head back or altering your posture in some other way when you take a breath?
- Is your diaphragm moving freely?
- Are your belly muscles supporting your breath?
- Are you holding your breath in between thoughts when you pause or using those moments to refuel your breath?

The answers to these questions will provide a list of your tension patterns and how these are getting in the way of your public speaking.

For my clients, I demonstrate and explain how breathing works naturally, making sure that they understand this on a visual and kinaesthetic level. Awareness always comes first. We then explore how to access a more advantageous breathing system. During this process, we work with whatever comes up, letting patterns go and establishing new ones.

When you breathe consciously, you are breathing into your back, lower ribs and belly. There is no need to arch your back to take in more air or to puff out your upper chest. Your lower ribs are not connected in the front of your body and so they have a great capacity for extension. This allows the diaphragm to fully flexion and the lower lungs to fill up with air as you breathe.

Change often comes through thinking and feeling kinaesthetically, which allows you to breathe more deeply into your body, your belly and your pelvic floor. This allows your belly muscles to move forward when you breathe in (which may feel counterintuitive, especially if you are used to holding your belly in).

FOUNDATIONAL BREATHING
EXERCISES FOR YOUR VOICE

There are numerous breathing exercises, many of which use the breath to achieve certain results. The exercises here are foundational and specifically designed to support your speaking voice by enabling you to:

- develop an awareness of how your voice functions as an instrument
- understand how to lessen tension so you may breathe easier
- learn to develop the capacity and support of your breath.

During all these exercises, notice the connection between your posture and your breath. Notice how letting go of tension, and finding length and width in your back, opens your body up and enables it to participate in your breath.

Many emotions may emerge during breathing exercises as you release tension and bring awareness to your experience. You may feel more vulnerable or you may feel a tremendous relief from simply letting your breathing fully happen. While emotions may arise, keep your awareness on the experience of the breath and your body. If you feel overwhelmed, bring more awareness into the room, the space where you are and your contact with the floor. Let this ground you.

Balanced, centred and supported breathing also help to centre our emotional lives. Relate to these emotions as part of the atmosphere, rather than the entire scene. This helps you to actually experience them instead of reacting to them.

These four exercises include a warm-up that is excellent to use before all other resonance, articulation and delivery practices, as well as before presentations.

EXERCISE 14
RELAXING INTO YOUR BREATH
Duration: 5–10 minutes

**PURPOSE: INCREASE YOUR AWARENESS IN
PREPARATION FOR THE NEXT EXERCISE**

Start in a semi-supine or seated position. As is most evident when you sleep, in this position you can breathe without needing any conscious attention.

Here you are going to navigate the space between autopilot and active change. You are going to work indirectly through a process of developing awareness and thereby getting out of the way.

STEP 1

Bring your awareness to your breath without changing anything or altering it in anyway. Simply notice the movement of your breath. Notice the length of the inhale and exhale, any sensations as you breathe and any change from breath to breath. Notice the movements of your torso.

STEP 2

As you notice any tensions, limitations or discomfort, let them go and resist the urge to 'fix' your breath or force it into a specific 'correct' or desirable pattern.

For instance, if you are clenching your jaw, gently let your teeth separate and your jaw soften. Notice how this impacts your breath.

Are you holding your back and lower ribs? Let them go and let your diaphragm drop.

Are you tightening your lower belly?

Observe how the release of tension (which inhibits movement and connectivity) allows your breath to move more deeply into your body.

Allow your posture to accommodate these changes. This may feel like an unwinding or peeling away of layers.

EXERCISE 15

THE CONTROLLED BREATH
Duration: 10 minutes

PURPOSE: INCREASE YOUR BREATH CAPACITY IN PREPARATION FOR SPEAKING

This exercise builds on Exercise 14. It guides you to fully fuel your voice for speech while reducing any adrenaline rush or nerves. Lie on your back in the semi-supine position (see Exercise 11).

Step 1: Do nothing. Come to a complete stop. You have nowhere else to be other than in this moment, breathing.

Step 2: Notice how your back feels on the floor or bed, and notice which parts of your body move when you inhale and when you exhale.

Step 3: Allow air into your lungs through your nose. This will help to increase your rib expansion. Part your lips and allow your exhalation to move freely through your lips. Repeat this cycle for three minutes.

At this point you should be feeling relaxed and can begin the process of increasing your breath intake.

Step 4: Pull your belly muscles in, expel air and pause for two seconds with a gentle hold of your breath. *(Note: Do not hold or tense your throat.)*

Step 5: Release your belly and allow air to fill your lungs, causing your lower ribcage to expand. Pause for two seconds.

Step 6: Sound an 'S' as the air escapes. Pause for two seconds. Notice how the 'S' sound further activates your belly muscles to pull in and expel air. Out of all the fricative (long sustained) consonants, 'S' lets out the least amount of air. It requires air to be pushed through your teeth. More resistance naturally encourages more breath support.

Step 7: Release your belly and allow air to fill your lungs. When breath comes in, you will find that you can automatically take in more.

Repeat: Repeat the 'S' exhale, pause, allow an automatic inhale, pause and so on.

Continue this exercise for ten minutes.

Note: During the exercise, revisit Step 2 throughout the exercise. Scan your body and make sure you are not tensing your muscles while you breathe in and out. If you are pressed for time, think quality not quantity. The exercise can be done in five minutes, provided you do not skip Steps 1 and 2. Make sure you stay in the moment, just as you would if you were speaking.

EXERCISE 16
INCREASE BREATH SUPPORT
Duration: 5 minutes

PURPOSE: INCREASE THE VOLUME OF YOUR VOICE

This exercise should be done standing. If you have a large mirror, stand in front of it and watch the movement of your torso. Scan your body throughout the exercise to make sure you are not tightening your throat, neck or chest. This exercise should make you feel relaxed, powerful and grounded.

Step 1: Do nothing. Come to a complete stop. You have nowhere else to be other than in this moment, breathing.

Step 2: Stand with your feet hip-width apart, knees relaxed and tailbone pointed towards the floor.

Step 3: Allow air into your lungs through your nose and out through your mouth.

Step 4: Relax your belly muscles. These are your vocal support muscles and they increase your volume (loudness) when speaking.

Step 5: Take in a deeper breath and roll a long 'R' with your tongue. If this is difficult, blow air through your lips like you are creating the sound of a motorcycle. The first time the sound should last five to eight seconds. The second, third, and fourth times the sound should last ten seconds. If you are not reaching ten seconds, you need more air. The way to achieve more air is to relax your belly muscles when you breathe in so your diaphragm can move down, creating extra space for your lungs to fill with air.

Step 6: Say "yes" and forcefully pull your belly muscles to your spine, then relax, allowing your belly to pop back out. Try to isolate the movement to your belly only. The belly muscles go towards your spine while you speak and relax when you are silent. Repeat this three times then relax and scan your body.

Repeat the exercise three times (until you have sounded the word "yes" a total of nine times).

EXERCISE 17
DAILY LIFE – SUPPORT IS NORMAL
Duration: 2–3 minutes a few times a day

**PURPOSE: CONDITION YOURSELF
TO HAVE BREATH SUPPORT DAILY**

Bring the notion and experience of support to your daily speech interactions.

Actively think about your voice and let it be supported. Gradually this will become natural.

You will find that your thoughts, emotions, breath support and sound begin to link into one fluid action.

YOGIC BREATHING AND OTHER
SPECIAL BREATH PRACTICES

There are many different breathing practices with specific goals. In general, the questions you need to ask are:
- What is the purpose of this breathing exercise?
- Does this breathing exercise support voice and speech?

For instance, I've collaborated with yoga practitioners who work with Ujjayi breath. One of the main intentions of this kind of breath is to build up heat in the body, which is valuable for the work done in the yoga poses. It is not helpful for speech. It sends a lot of air onto the vocal folds, which tends to dry them out. The folds need to be lubricated all the time while speaking or the chance of vocal damage increases.

The first goal of all voice and speech breathing exercises is to eliminate unnecessary tension and to restore access to natural breathing. If you have strong habits that interfere with your natural breathing capacities, you bring those habits to any special exercise you do.

Establish a healthy, strong natural breath for your voice. Then, be clear about the purpose behind any special breathing technique and apply it accordingly. When you are not doing those exercises, return to your natural supported breath.

7.
Resonance

———

Increasing the Richness
of Your Voice

———

*"What was going on between us created
a resonance that goes beyond the music itself."*
Lindsey Buckingham, Fleetwood Mac

While your breath is essential for creating and supporting the sound you make, your breath does not carry the sound to your audience. The sound is a wave of vibration that may travel through many different media – primarily, for a speaker, through the air.

The biggest obstacles to voice production are believing that:

- you need to strain yourself to speak loudly
- you need to force your breath through your throat
- you need to use any kind of strain in your vocal tract or body in general.

Clients tell me they need to project their voice, yet this idea carries with it the idea of tension and effort.

You can resolve these tendencies through clarifying your understanding of how sound is produced, and training yourself to experience a harmonious coordination of your voice.

In voice and speech training, projection is called 'resonance'. It's rare that a speaker doesn't need to increase the resonant sound of their voice. There are some natural speakers who, with little effort, create beautiful sound. However, this is not the case for most of us.

By developing and relying on your resonating capacity, you avoid causing vocal fatigue and strain in your voice. You can be heard. You gain the ease and poise of aligning your sound-making with your extraordinary anatomy, rather than working against it. You also receive the energizing and relaxing benefits of this 'inner vibrating current', as described by one of the most respected voice training innovators of the last century, Arthur Lessac, in *The Use and Training of the Human Voice*.

Lessac suggests that resonance has a certain magical quality. Learning about and activating your resonating capacities will change your experience of your body. You will discover that it is a resonating chamber composed of many different resonating structures and spaces. In addition, attuning to resonance can further develop your experience of sound in general, how it travels, and how the design of a room impacts the quality of the sound and the audience's listening attention.

THE THREE KINDS OF RESONANCE

Phonation is the physical act of making vocal sound. In an instant – triggered by an impulse from the brain – air passes through the vocal folds at a speed and pressure that stimulate the folds to move together and apart. The oscillation of the folds creates sound waves.

From its origins (the vocal folds), sound resonates through the whole vocal tract (the throat and the oral and nasal cavities), becoming amplified on its way out of the speaker and into the listener's ears. When the sound is further shaped by the articulators (tongue, jaw and lips), we recognize it as speech. This is known as 'primary resonance'.

'Secondary resonance' is the vibration, caused simultaneously by the vocal folds, that travels through your bones and other tissues into your inner ear. This is also known as 'bone conduction'.

Both primary and secondary resonance occur when you speak. If you've ever wondered why you sound different when you're recorded from how you do when listening to yourself live, this is the reason. Your ear is experiencing primary and secondary resonance simultaneously. The sound you hear is a richer, deeper sound than what is heard by the outside world.

Over the page is an expert from *When Listening Comes Alive* which speaks to secondary resonance.

As the eardrum is completely immersed in liquid, it cannot pick up or transmit any vibration. Thus, the only way the sound can reach the ear of the child-to-be-born is through bone conduction. To hear his mother's voice by bone conduction, he puts his body against the spinal column, a column of sound. That way he is directly 'plugged in' to the voice. Towards the end of pregnancy, he puts his head down against the hip bones of the mother, which became his own private auditorium at the bottom of the spine.
(Paul Madaule, *When Listening Comes Alive*)

Our experience of sonic resonance is fundamental to our experience of life and connection. It follows that these resonances have essential benefits for you and your audience.

This emotional resonance is something most people have experienced at the sound of a specific voice or song. The exact mechanism is a subject of debate. Some do not believe emotional resonance is connected to the physical vibrations of sound waves. However, in my opinion, regardless of the exact mechanism, as a speaker either you believe you have the power through your voice to emotionally sway an audience or you don't. If you choose to believe in your own vocal power, you open the door to many possibilities for affecting your audience.

WHAT GETS IN THE WAY
OF THE QUALITY OF
OUR RESONANCE?

From childhood through to adulthood, you will have been inundated with messaging requesting you to be quiet, use an 'inside voice' and fit in with others. This causes many people to make their presence 'smaller' in order to fit into society's norms, which often involves compromising their voice. The degree of compromise varies, depending on cultural influences, attitudes at school and attitudes at home. But some degree of compromise often exists.

To overcome such influences, you need to give yourself the space, place and time to explore your voices. A richly resonant voice is accessible to everyone. Learning to internally feel resonance is the critical method for activating it. Resonance exercises must be fuelled with a well-supported breath and well-coordinated posture. By committing to exercises and by bringing resonance into your conversations and presentations, you can practise this on a regular basis.

As you explore the exercises that follow, you will experience yourself as a resonating chamber.

Take your time to undo any excess tension before you begin and to establish a centred, tidal breath. Notice, as you do the exercises, whether any tension creeps in – especially around your neck, jaw and throat. Freely take a pause, release the tension and resume when you are ready.

I highly recommended using a mirror or, occasionally, a video recording to simply observe what is happening and any patterns that show up – for example, pulling your head back or arching your spine. Use your awareness to undo, from the inside out, any tendencies to disconnect.

The best attitude here is one of curiosity and fun. This approach does not make your old way wrong. It simply opens up new possibilities.

But, at the same time, be sure not to confuse what's optimal with what's perfect or beautiful. Resonance is not about making your voice perfect or fitting into an idea of what is beautiful. It's about being free of tension and letting your voice naturally emerge in all its character, range and colour.

The goals here are firstly to understand and experience resonance, secondly to increase the resonant sound of your voice and finally to integrate resonance more fully into your public speaking and speaking in daily life.

Developing resonating capacity to its very fullest is fundamental for singers – from Freddie Mercury to Amy Winehouse to Pavarotti. Similarly, in classical music, Mozart was an absolute genius for weaving together the many resonant frequencies. His music is used in listening therapy programs throughout the world to activate and restore the ear's full functioning.

Public speakers are generally not recognized and celebrated to the same degree for their resonance skill. Yet, there are speakers who show tremendous virtuosity and who move us with the qualities within their voices, such as James Earl Jones, Morgan Freeman and Katharine Hepburn.

Listen to Sir Laurence Olivier perform as Hamlet. He is not particularly emotive or manipulative with his acting. He simply mastered Shakespeare by understanding the text and fine-tuning his instrument. As you listen, and hopefully watch, you see an actor with little to no excess tension in his way of producing heightened Elizabethan text. He makes it look easy.

Michelle Obama is another great example of a resonant voice. Most people can listen to Michelle Obama for hours and stay captivated. There are other factors of course. She is highly intelligent and articulate. But underneath the articulation is resonance. This will dictate how you feel about a speaker on a fundamental level. We don't struggle to listen to her. She is loud, clear, calm and relaxed; her energy goes into her voice, instead of being used up by tension. Notice how your body feels while she speaks.

Note: To avoid straining or damaging your voice, be sure to release any excess tension in your neck, chest and belly before you try the resonance and articulation exercises in this chapter (see the section 'Alexander Technique' in Chapter 5 for further details).

EXERCISE 18
INCREASE VOCAL RESONANCE
Duration: 10 minutes

PURPOSE: BE HEARD WITHOUT STRAINING

This exercise and Exercise 19 can be used as daily practice and as warm-ups, after breath work and before speaking.

Start this exercise lying on your back in the semi-supine position (see Exercise 11) with your eyes open, letting your breath calm and centred.

Step 1: Do nothing. Come to a complete stop. You have nowhere else to be other than in this moment, breathing.

Step 2: Notice how your back feels on the floor or table. Notice which parts of your body move when you inhale and when you exhale.

Step 3: Allow air into your lungs through your nose. This will help to increase your rib expansion. Part your lips and allow your exhalation to move freely through your lips for three minutes.

At this point you should be feeling relaxed and can begin the process of increasing your breath intake.

Step 4: Pull your belly muscles in, expel air and pause for two seconds.

Step 5: Release your belly and allow air to fill your lungs, causing your lower ribcage to expand. Pause for two seconds. Sound an 'S' to more fully activate your breathing support muscles as the air escapes.

Note: During the exercise, revisit Step 2 continually throughout the exercise. Scan your body and make sure you are not tensing your muscles as you continue to breathe in and out.

Step 6: Release your belly and allow air to fill your lungs, causing your lower ribcage to expand. Pause for two seconds. Sound a 'Z' as the air escapes. Repeat five times, returning to tidal breath when needed.

This exercise should last 10 minutes. If you are pressed for time, think quality not quantity. The exercise can be done in seven minutes, provided you do not skip Steps 1 and 2. Make sure you stay in the moment just as you would when speaking.

Step 7: Stand and repeat Step 1 and Step 6.

Step 8: Speak. You can use your elevator pitch, poetry or lyrics. Notice how your voice is sounding clear and strong. Recording yourself before and after the exercise will help to motivate you to practise.

EXERCISE 19
EXPLORE RESONATING CHAMBERS
Duration: 5 minutes

PURPOSE: INCREASE THE RICHNESS AND MELODIC QUALITY OF YOUR SOUND

Start with Steps 1–6 of Exercise 18. Stay in the semi-supine position to start.

Step 1: Do nothing. Come to a complete stop. You have nowhere else to be other than in this moment. Now stand with your feet hip-width apart, knees relaxed. Standing in front of a mirror is optimal.

Step 2: Fill your lungs with air and sound 'ZH', as in the sound made in 'measure'. Feel the sound waves vibrating the gum ridge and the front of your teeth. Next, fill your lungs with air and sound an 'E' as in 'heat'. Think of sending the sound waves through your teeth. Touch your face and notice most of the vibrations are coming through the oral cavity.

Step 3: Sound an 'E' as in 'heat' high into your head. Place a hand on your forehead and feel the vibrations.

Step 4: Sound an 'E' as in 'heat' low into your chest. Place a hand on your chest below your collarbone and feel the vibrations.

Step 5: Sound an 'E' as in 'heat' low into your throat. Place a hand on your larynx. Make sure you are not tilting your head back. Feel the vibrations.

Step 6: Sound an 'E' as in 'heat' into your nose. Touch the top and sides of your nose so you can feel your nasal cavity vibrating.

Which are easy to access? Which are more difficult?

Which seem to drop out or deactivate when you speak?

EXERCISE 20
EXPLORING RESONANCE IN SPEECH
Duration: Depends on speech length

PURPOSE: CREATE A RICHER SOUND

Now that you've explored and experienced the felt sensations of resonance, the next step is to explore the experience in your speech.

Explore the techniques in Exercise 19 with your own text and note how much more resonant you sound having accessed more resonating chambers.

8.
Articulation

Shaping Sound
to Be Heard

"Speak clearly, if you speak at all;
carve every word before you let it fall."
Oliver Wendell Holmes, *Urania: A Rhymed Lesson*

Breath helps us focus.

Resonance helps us feel.

Articulation helps us understand.

This is my favourite aspect of physical training. I love it, most likely because I lack patience. The most dramatic shift in performance happens when a speaker with slurred or lazy articulation sharpens to razor-like perfection.

Articulation is the physical act of shaping sound. It involves a symphony of complex coordinated muscular actions made by our lips, tongue, facial muscles, jaw and soft palate.

We are deeply programmed articulators. At the beginning of our lives, we don't so much learn as we activate the innate. Just as with crawling and walking, babies naturally go through stages, developing the muscles and subtle coordination necessary to shape their words. Before we know it, and our parents can hardly believe it, the sound play has graduated into "mama" and "papa" (or something entirely unexpected) – with many more words soon to follow.

Your articulation is further developed and limited by your personal physiology, experience and culture. You are in a constant feedback loop of hearing and speaking.

WHEN IT COMES TO PUBLIC SPEAKING, NEVER UNDERESTIMATE THE POWER OF ARTICULATION

For you, it brings energy and clarity into your voice. The activation and coordination of your articulators enlivens your brain and can brighten your thinking and entire delivery.

Consider a dull voice and how this reflects in your whole body.

At the same time, an audience that is straining to understand is likely to be less receptive and available. You are asking something of them, on a physical level, that is directly interfering with the purpose you have for speaking to them. Clear articulation enables your audience to receive your content. It communicates clear thinking and confidence.

When it comes to great public speakers or great speeches, the one noticeable commonality is a clear, crisp vibrant articulation. I say noticeable because if you were to watch John F. Kennedy's inaugural address, or Martin Luther King's "I Have a Dream", you would not likely notice their breathing, but you would notice their articulation in the clarity of their expression. You might also notice that listening to a speaker who takes their time to clearly articulate their words allows you to relax.

THE ART OF SHAPING SOUND:
LISTEN, FEEL, WATCH

My first articulation class was part of the Royal Academy of Dramatic Arts (RADA) Shakespeare program in London, which I attended at the age of 25. I hated the class.

One day, I watched the teacher in dismay: how could anyone choose this as a profession? We had just spent ten minutes on the word 'door'. The teacher insisted that the Americans in the class pronounced it as 'daaww' and was showing quite a bit of frustration at our lack of ability to mimic her in shaping a sound that doesn't exist in the American accent. After ten minutes, 21-year-old Julia from Tennessee blurted out, "Look lady, it's a door with an 'R'. We don't even have that 'daaww' sound in America. Why should we pronounce it that way?"

I quietly began to laugh and, even though I tried to keep my composure, I could not. Julia and I both failed the class.

My 'dawww' failure aside, what I learned in that class greatly shaped how I teach articulation. Over the past decade, I've tested and brought these insights to clients worldwide.

First and foremost, I learned what not to do. Practising the fundamentals of articulation is different from learning how to speak a specific accent. The teacher at RADA, despite being well trained, was basing her general articulation exercises on a specific accent. She was trying to get us to speak Received Pronunciation, also known as the Standard English accent in the UK. We have our own 'standard' in the US, called General American. The teacher's efforts were unnecessary, and asking students to do something that has absolutely no use for them is only discouraging.

You can improve your articulation while speaking in your primary accent. This will clarify your speech and help you be understood regardless of your accent. Reducing or developing an accent is a more specialized type of training with a different goal.

ARTICULATION EXERCISES

Articulation exercises are very physical workouts. If done correctly, they can completely alter an audience's perception of you.

I highly recommend recording yourself or using a mirror when using the exercises in this chapter, in particular Exercise 21: Prop It Open and Exercise 24: Clarity and Emotion, as these two are more challenging. These are also excellent warm-ups to use prior to speeches. It is important to remember to breathe and relax. Excess tension from trying to do the exercise 'right' can stiffen your tongue and tighten your jaw.

Take a playful attitude, and let the process of repetition and exploration rewire and refine your brain–speech pathways. It's easy to get twisted up, but it's just as easy to untwist, let go and play again. You'll eventually hear the pay-off.

The first step is to establish the new movement. Notice where you are stumbling and where things feel easy. Notice whether tension creeps into your throat, jaw or posture, and keep coming back to neutral. Often, as we engage lazy or under-activated muscles – the tongue, the lips, the many muscles of the face – they commandeer a host of other structures from the jaw to the shoulders to the feet. Part of the work is undoing these patterns to find freer action and new connections.

As you find the coordination – the new pattern – you want to strengthen it through repetition in exercises and daily use, until it's natural. If you are struggling, slow down, refresh the ease and balance in your posture, and re-establish the support in your breath.

There is an endless number of possible exercises for articulation. The ones here cover what I feel are the essentials in a direct, fun way with enough variety that you will be able to gauge your strengths and weaknesses.

Note: To avoid straining or damaging your voice, be sure to release any excess tension in your neck, chest and belly before you try the resonance and articulation exercises in this chapter (see the section 'Alexander Technique' in Chapter 5 for further details).

EXERCISE 21

PROP IT OPEN

Duration: 10 minutes

PURPOSE: QUICKLY IMPROVE ARTICULATION

This exercise encourages the lips and tongue to shape sound aggressively by inhibiting the movement of the jaw.

Select a text for your initial practice. I prefer to use poetry or a section of a speech I am preparing to deliver.

Put a mint in between your teeth. Relax your jaw as opposed to biting down.

Read the text in front of a mirror one sentence at a time.

Exaggerate the use of your lips and your tongue tip. Think of the tip of your tongue as a drumstick and your gum ridge as the drum. Hit it with force and precision. Think of your lips as if they were trying to leave your face, shaping sound out in front of your teeth.

Make sure you are breathing effortlessly.

Notice when your jaw engages or when tension creeps in from anywhere – your throat, chest, jaw, etc. Letting this tension go, in order to fully activate and free your tongue and lips, is a key purpose of this exercise.

If you find that you are repeatedly tensing your jaw or elsewhere, stop for a moment. Take the mint out.

Take a moment to breathe and recentre, then replace the mint and start again.

Record yourself reading a few lines before you start the exercise and after the exercise is over, so you can hear the result.

When I do this exercise with clients, they have the added benefit of mimicking me, then looking in the mirror to compare the use of their articulators. They often think they are doing something enough when the reality is that they are not. For this reason, I suggest you really explore the movements, even if you feel you are exaggerating. Just keep breathing with good support. And if you feel like it's a real workout, it is!

EXERCISE 22
TONGUE AGILITY
Duration: 10 minutes

PURPOSE: STRENGTHEN TONGUE-TIP
CONSONANT SOUNDS

This exercise encourages you to be precise in how the tip of your tongue touches your gum ridge when you form the consonants 'T' and 'D', and in how the tip of your tongue touches your teeth for the consonant sound 'TH'.

Before you do this exercise, say the following: "My 27th birthday was three days ago. Thirty-three dark days." Notice how the tip of your tongue moves.

Pronounce the vowels as follows: AH as in 'dark', OH as in 'ago', AY as in 'day' and EE as in 'three'. Separate the sounds AH-T-TH as indicated by the hyphen. Do not run them together.

Voiced consonants are consonants that are formed using both sound waves and air: B, D, G, TH, V, DG, N, M and Z. If you are unclear as to what is voiced or unvoiced, gently touch your Adam's apple while making the sound. If it is voiced it will vibrate; if unvoiced, it will not vibrate.

Unvoiced consonants are sounded with air only: P, T, K, TH, F, H, CH and S.

AH-T-TH, OH-T-TH, AY-T-TH, EE-T-TH
(TH is unvoiced as in 'think')

AH-D-TH, OH-D-TH, AY-D-TH, EE-D-TH
(TH is voiced as in 'this')

AH-TH-T, OH-TH-T, AY-TH-T, EE-TH-T
(TH is unvoiced as in 'think')
AH-TH-D, OH-TH-D, AY-TH-D, EE-DT-H
(TH is voiced as in 'this')

After you do this exercise, say the following again: "My 27th birthday was three days ago. Thirty-three dark days." Note the difference.

If you stumble here or feel a wave of sudden frustration while attempting to make the sounds, approach the exercise more playfully. Think of it as a coordination practice, like learning a dance step.

As you practice, you are waking up your nervous system as much as your tongue.

EXERCISE 23
TONGUE TWISTERS
Duration: 5–10 minutes

**PURPOSE: INCREASE AGILITY FOR
THE TONGUE AND LIPS**

Tongue twisters encourage the lips and tongue to be precise when forming vowels and consonants while opening the jaw for the appropriate movement for vowels. Each tongue twister trains different skills, just as you might do a variety of weightlifting exercises or yoga postures to get the different aspects of your physique in shape and working together.

For each tongue twister, start by articulating the pattern and then work towards stamina and integration at any speed. Especially train the ones that are the most challenging for you while maintaining breath support. You can also use these as warm-ups.

TONGUE TWISTER 1
Repeat this three times slowly and then three times quickly:
Red Leather Yellow Leather
Notice the precision of the tongue tip on the gum ridge for D and L, then the fast flicker of the tongue for TH.

TONGUE TWISTER 2
Repeat this three times slowly and then three times quickly:
Peggy Babcock
Notice the lips for P and B coordinating with the back of tongue for G and K. Made sure your jaw opens for the /ei/ diphthong "Peg" and /ae/ open vowel "Bab".

TONGUE TWISTER 3

Repeat this twice:

Whether the weather be cold or whether the weather be hot, we'll weather the weather whatever the weather, whether we like it or not.

Exaggerate the movement of your lips back and forth. Notice the tongue pulling back into the mouth from the TH position into ER and lips moving back out for R.

TONGUE TWISTER 4

Repeat this twice:

Every sea anemone has an enemy anemone.

EXERCISE 24
CLARITY AND EMOTION
Duration: 10 minutes

PURPOSE: DISCOVER HOW ARTICULATION
CONVEYS EMOTION

This is an advanced exercise. I suggest trying the others first to build up your skills. In acting training, it is said, "Consonants carry clarity, vowels carry emotion." We need both to be heard and felt, and this exercise will help you to clearly articulate both.

Select a text. Poetry works best. To start, I offer you the poem my mother wrote while she looked at me in my receiving blanket right after I was born.

From the icy mouth of winter came a baby's cry
A word of summer bringings
Dreams that flutter by
December sighs in silence
As bobbles if icelets flow
The world has donned in elegance
A proper ermine robe

Read the text out loud once to familiarize yourself with it. Now underline all the spoken consonants in the speech. If a consonant is silent, like the L in walk, skip it. Then read the text again, pronouncing only all the **consonants** out loud exactly as they would be pronounced in the word. So 'C' in 'icy' is a 'S' sound while 'C' in 'cry' is a 'K'. Do not pronounce any vowels. Repeat this a few times, and play with the drum-set quality of the rhythm and sound.

> Then articulate only the **vowels** as they would be pronounced in the words. Do not pronounce any consonants.
>
> People typically feel that one of these exercises (consonants or vowels) is more difficult than the other. Which was more difficult for you?
>
> After you've practised with your selected text, do the exercise again with another speech, a talk or a pitch you are working on.

CONSIDERING ... VOWELS AND CONSONANTS

Vowels and consonants emerge at different times in our development as young children. Our experiences in those times may be reflected in how we relate to this and other articulation exercises. As we practise, we are building on our earliest sound and word play, which later become communication and the assimilation of language.

When we are three- to five-month-old infants, we use only vowel sounds to communicate. Being limited to only the use of vowels to communicate during the exercise can increase any feelings of vulnerability, and even helplessness, as it subconsciously reminds us of being completely dependent on caregivers for survival. If you carry a lot of vulnerability, you may find the vowel exercise more difficult.

Consonants are introduced around the age of one to two years. We have already started walking at that point, are less vulnerable and are more concerned with precision. Therefore, people who find the consonant exercise harder tend to lean towards perfectionism.

I encourage you to try this exercise a few times, even if it seems difficult. After the exercise, record yourself reading the entire text, and the pay-off should be noticeable. Your consonants should be crisp and your vowels rich. Great articulation separates the novice and the master.

Part Three

Delivery

*"All the world's a stage, and all the men
and women merely players."*
William Shakespeare, *As You Like It*

This part of the book contains the foundations of great stage presence and delivery that theatre artists and directors have used for decades. I approach this work very much in the same way a voice and text coach approaches Shakespeare. By exploring how we inspire people through the use of language, we discover that language carries power. Using it well brings out the life in your speech and can encourage an audience to really listen and to stay with you. I've included elements of delivery technique that have the greatest impact – for example, working with pauses, fleshing out imagery words and matching the meaning of the words with your emotional tone.

Additionally, in this part of the book, we investigate the power of listening, storytelling, memorization, and adapting content and delivery to suit various settings.

I encourage you to review the material in each chapter and familiarize yourself with the exercises. Use the principles and techniques to work on your speeches. Rehearse regularly, as the many great speakers and actors through the centuries have. Watch and listen to yourself on recordings. Review your presentations and select areas where you'd like to improve. If you feel stuck or frustrated, do the exercises in Part Two to open your voice and relax your mind. Consider whether you are placing expectation or false beliefs on yourself where curiosity is needed. Get accustomed to returning to your purpose and your breath as you deliver your message to others.

9.

Purpose
And Setting

———

Why Are You Speaking and
Whom Are You Speaking to?

———

*"Getting an audience is hard. Sustaining an audience is hard.
It demands a consistency of thought, of purpose,
and of action over a long period of time."*
Bruce Springsteen

A few years ago, I was helping a client prepare for her first TED Talk. Rose was extremely excited as she knew this would give her the exposure necessary to boost her career as a professional public speaker. She showed up to the first session with 90% of her content in place and ready to work on delivery.

Her dedication to her work and enthusiasm to share it were clear in her content and delivery. Yet, as she spoke, I was not listening to her. I was simply analysing her performance. After a run-through of her 12-minute talk, I asked her, "Why are you speaking?" She answered, "Because I want exposure so I can book paid speaking jobs. I really want to hit this out of the park." This was a reasonable answer as to why Rose accepted the invitation to speak. However, it was not enough for a delivery that would "hit it out of the park".

I asked my question three more times. Rose finally got it. "I'm speaking because as a country we need to look at criminal justice in a different way. We need to start seeing criminal justice as rehabilitation, not punishment." Once she was grounded in her reason to speak, we were able to craft her delivery and hone her message. This required some cutting of text that was distracting from her core message, as she hadn't had her purpose in place when she'd written the script. Then we applied pacing and word stress techniques (described in Chapters 10 and 11). By the end of the hour, I was no longer analysing Rose's performance. I was listening intently to every word she said.

Now is a good time to pause and think about the great speeches you've heard and what made them great. It is likely that these speeches were about something bigger than the speaker and the audience. They resonated with the audience because the speaker was focusing on the greater good, not on themselves or a personal or professional gain.

Focus can make or break your speech. Start by making an intellectual connection with your purpose (reason) for speaking, and think more deeply about the audience and the setting. Who are you speaking to and what do you want the audience to do with the information you are sharing? Simplicity is important here. Define what you want and why.

New speakers, and even a fair share of seasoned ones, tend to be more focused on themselves than their message: How do I look? How do I sound? Was I good? These are common questions and, to some extent, it is understandable that speakers will ask them. New speakers are learning the terrain, in need of practice and looking for feedback. Constructive feedback is a good thing. It is how you gain insight into your delivery and how to hone your message.

However, focusing on yourself during your speech compromises your relationship to your audience. The audience will find it harder to listen to you for a long period of time and stay engaged. It sets you up for disappointment, and by over-focusing on yourself you are disconnecting from your bigger objectives.

Consider the purpose of the overall event and why you are being asked to speak. Perhaps because you are an expert? Because you have a personal story to tell that is relevant to the overall event? Because your purpose matches the overall point of the conference?

You will often not be the only speaker at an event. Ask the event organizer where you fit in and how what you are offering this audience will be different from what the other speakers are offering. Why is it important that the audience hears what you have to say in this time and place? What can you give the audience? For instance, if you are at a rally, you will want them to consider voting differently, or to educate or motivate them about an important initiative. What is going to motivate the audience into taking action?

If you are speaking to get exposure for one reason or another, you still need the focus to be on the content of your speech. You need to educate, to influence, to share something of value and relevance that is not about you. In short, focus on the objectives you can control that are most alive for you and your audience.

I suggest keeping these principles in mind when speaking to any audience, large or small. This includes giving quarterly reports to your team or board members, showing design options to engineering teams, conducting weekly meetings and so forth.

Write down your potential objectives, and then take a moment to consider each. Think about whether the objectives are achievable. Which outcomes can you control, and which can you not control? Let go of the objectives you have no control over, such as wanting to dazzle the audience, getting people to hire you or making people like you – these outcomes are largely beyond your control. What you can control is whether you articulate your message clearly, and physical aspects such as your pacing and breathing. By choosing achievable goals, you will be able to speak with relaxed confidence.

AN ACTOR'S OBJECTIVE, A SPEAKER'S PURPOSE

An actor's job is to understand what the playwright is saying about the human condition and what their character's role is in expressing this message. Through reading, analysing and rehearsing a script, the actor ensures this understanding informs every scene, line, movement and interaction.

This understanding is the root that powers an actor's performance and heightens their presence.

A speaker, similarly, needs to consider their personal purpose, the overall purpose of the particular speaking event and their role within it. We all have intentions and worldviews, consciously and unconsciously, embedded in everything we do. A speaker's purpose may come from a deeply personal place. It may also come from a vocational mission, from a job requirement or from a role within an organization. The deeply personal often informs the professional. Often, there are many purposes driving a speech. The clearer you are with yourself regarding your personal and professional objectives, the better your content and delivery will serve your aims.

Sometimes you simply know your purpose, like a doctor who is an expert who's been invited to speak at a conference in her field. She is there to educate the audience and give them tools and insights to help them perform their work.

Sometimes you will need to consider the situation, or what is most important to you at that time. You may consider asking the curators of the event to share what they are most interested in about your work or story. Some speakers reach out to audience members or people directly in their networks to ask them to suggest or highlight topics they would like to hear about. Finally, trusted friends, family, colleagues and mentors may have insights or can be sounding boards for your ideas.

PEELING BACK PURPOSE:
TED TALKS AND
'SPREADING IDEAS'

TED has grown to be one of the most watched conferences worldwide. The audience is there because they choose to be. They are brought by the idea that they will learn something.

That learning gives them hope in their personal development and desire to change how they relate to themselves, others and solutions to societal issues. TED Talks can be extremely educational and inspiring. The guidelines for TED conferences offer a very useful strategy for a speaker to use to peel back the layers of purpose.

The guidelines for a TED speaker are strict. Any self, product or company promotion is prohibited. It's the idea that dominates, not the person or company. This is what has made TED so successful. It challenges speakers to dig deeper into their purpose in order to deliver meaningful, rich content. It is no surprise that this often brings a strong personal element to TED Talks.

While on the committee at TEDxSF, I had to cut the scripts of several speakers. Some speakers were very surprised I wouldn't let them mention their company's name. By stripping away promotion of any kind, all we had left was storytelling, through which we asked the audience to think differently about a particular subject. The audiences were enthusiastic and supportive. The speakers were able to ground themselves in their purpose for being at the event.

We will return to explore types of TED Talk more deeply in the next chapter, "Storytelling and Structure". For now, the message from TED is that you can learn a lot from stripping away your agenda and focus on storytelling. You may not be preparing a TED Talk, but you can use the philosophy behind it to dig deeper into what drives your speech.

ROLES WE PLAY

When Steve Jobs announced the iPhone, he was there to celebrate a revolutionary product and enjoyed his entire company cheering about the company's achievement. He was

Company Champion. This role was vastly different from the one he played at his famous commencement speech at Stanford, where he appeared as an Elder Mentor who encouraged the audience to "stay hungry stay foolish".

Let's imagine Jobs giving a toast at his daughter's wedding. There he would have been the father of the bride. His toast would have had a completely different tone – rich with intimate and personal feeling that expresses a father's love, offering congratulations and blessings.

We all play many different roles in life. We are friends, siblings, parents, colleagues, leaders, supporters, mentors, employees and so on. Each of these roles informs the way we communicate and the particular purposes we have in any one moment or situation. While we may give presentations in a particular role at work or a conference, we may offer a toast at a friend's retirement from a wholly different point of view and based on a completely different relationship with our audience.

So, when giving a speech, you should think about what role you are playing each time, for each situation. That is the persona you put on. This persona is not false – it is an expression appropriate to the situation. It is grounded in your life, and it comes from what you are expressing and why, not from something you are trying to pretend.

When you are aware of your role, you can embrace it and explore it fully. Consider the audience from the vantage point of this role. What is your message? What do you have to offer them? These questions can support you in generating the appropriate content for your speech, by enabling you to remain in that role during your speech and return to it readily in the future with more naturalness and ease.

PRESENTATION TYPES AND SETTINGS

Many speakers primarily offer one type of presentation in one setting. For instance, you may regularly present research or introduce new product developments at conferences. But you may very rarely give toasts or serve as an MC at a fundraising event. This section explores a range of presentations to consider how different settings may impact your delivery. Some content and delivery styles that may be great for one audience may fall flat or even alienate another.

ART PRESENTATIONS: THE CURATOR

I once worked with David, a curator who was about to present at a conference. He was very nervous about whether he was interesting or dynamic enough to hold the audience's attention. I saw that this was painful for him. He cared deeply about presenting the work and life history of the artist he was highlighting.

During the first run-through of the presentation, he was extremely self-conscious. His eyes stayed glued to the script he'd written, and his overall countenance seemed as if he were hiding. Like many sensitive people with high standards, however, he was talented. His content was strong and well thought out. And he had several slides from the artist's body of work that matched his content. Physically, he had a lovely resonant voice that needed very little work.

The recipe for a great delivery was there. All I needed to do was help David structure his presentation and ground him in his purpose for delivering it. The only thing truly standing in his way was his self-doubt.

We started by slowing down his breathing to reduce his nerves and allow him to better focus on the content of his speech. Then we started to shape his delivery by placing pauses where he could breathe and using body language to support his content. As we continued working, his confidence increased. A lovely presentation emerged from an educator backing the work of an artist. David's worry about being dynamic was misplaced and luckily disappeared. It wasn't his job to entertain, charm or persuade the audience with a showy delivery. His job was to articulate why this artist needed to be seen and to let the story he was telling, and his visual aids, do the work of pulling in the audience.

This kind of presentation style is the opposite of that of a politician, activist or salesperson. The delivery should not draw attention away from the subject and onto the speaker. If David did his job correctly, the audience should walk away thinking about the artist, not him. After I pointed this out, he was able to take the focus off himself and place it where it should be. This, and giving more structure to his content, reduced his nervousness and grounded him in his purpose.

A talk I saw by photographer James Mollison at TEDxSF Alive! in 2011 illustrates another important point about art presentations. Mollison presented on his work "Where Children Sleep", a series taken in the bedrooms of children from around the world to highlight the realities of living in either extreme poverty or extreme wealth.

The honesty in his delivery, coupled with powerful photos, left a lasting impression on me. Although I felt he could have benefited as a speaker from better posture, voice and speech training, his authentic delivery and care for the children he had photographed made his speech engaging. My take-away was the tragedy of isolation. Both wealthy and impoverished children were living lives of isolation, and in some respects already living in adulthood because they lacked time to play.

There was a slight disconnection between us (the audience) and Mollison (the speaker) as he spent the majority of the talk in profile watching the slides. Facing the audience now and then would have allowed the audience to be invited into the story, and to experience, to some degree, what James had experienced.

When you are the only one on stage or you are with what may be considered as 'dry data' on a screen, then holding your audience's attention with a more dynamic speaking style is appropriate. When you are showcasing an artist's work, you do not want to upstage your visuals because they are carrying your message as David's did. However, you still need to connect with your audience. Turn your body towards the audience and make eye contact whenever possible.

THE INVESTOR PITCH

In my private practice, I coach roughly 50 to 100 founders of start-ups a year. Typically, the CEO is responsible for pitching the start-up to investors. After initial seed money comes in from the founders, the rest of the funding is attained in three rounds: Series A, B and C. I am typically involved when a client is seeking to secure Series A funding. This kind of pitch is aimed at investors from venture capital firms. The pitch is typically two to four minutes in length, and the funding being sought is usually between $2 and $15 million.

Unless the founder is already well connected with investors, these pitches often happen through an accelerator program or at a contest. The programs are highly competitive to get into and it is often the case that a young founder is not a great speaker. The accelerators will help the CEO to practise their pitch, but it is rare for them to provide professional feedback. That is up to the start-up founder.

"I'm so happy to be named the winner today and I look forward to building the RangeMe marketplace and continuing to provide retailers with the right tools to be successful."
Nicky Jackson, CEO and Founder,
Winner of Digital Startup of the Year 2016,
National Retail Federation

Nicky was the first woman to receive entrance into this competition. Her director of marketing had met me through a networking event and introduced Nicky to me when he saw the high stakes of the competition were holding her back.

The pressure was causing her to speed up the rate of her speech. She was trying to put too much information into a short space of time. This was undermining her ability to create rapport with the audience.

Over two sessions, we worked together on applying pacing and pausing exercises, on slowing down and on only saying what was essential for the investors to hear. The result was a clear, concise and measured delivery, full of presence and leadership.

While Nicky certainly won the competition because her company was poised to fill a gap in the market, her delivery matched the strength of her business plan and highlighted its essentials.

In such situations, a founder has to build rapport with the audience. In a short pitch, they need to come across with status and leadership, and clearly articulate why this is the right company and right time to invest in it. That's a lot to accomplish in under four minutes. However, speed and trying to include every single thing are not the answer.

The audience – the investors and judges – are often very relaxed and confident; they are the ones with the money to invest. They are there to listen, and will primarily base their decision on your business plan, not on you. Poise, clarity of purpose and clear information that speaks directly to them will convey confidence and help them remember the essentials. The job of the founder is firstly not to get in the way of the message and secondly to highlight the key information the investors need to hear.

NON-PROFIT PRESENTATIONS

Typically, a representative of a non-profit speaks at a fundraiser or conference. At a fundraiser, the speaker appeals to the heart of the listener. The formula will usually contain a story, details about the success of the organization and a request for donations from the audience. In terms of the public speaking field, this is my favourite area of work.

In these situations, the purpose and setting for a speaker are generally very clear. Working for the greater good is an easy way to ground yourself in your purpose. Sharing success stories helps others to know you are doing the work that needs to be done without their hands-on involvement. The ask for donations is much easier if you've shared a poignant story.

I once coached Vidhu, a speaker for Change.org, who very effectively brought all these elements together. Vidhu was presenting a speech about a petition calling for the criminalization of burning women with acid in India. Just a few years ago, it was legal for a man to throw acid on a woman if she rejected his marriage proposal. A survivor of this type of attack started the petition, which Change.org then supported. Vidhu shared stories of victims of this practice. Then, she reported on how the petition eventually made it to the Indian government, which acted to outlaw this practice of revenge.

For most people, getting behind this petition would not be an issue. The practice is a horrific violation of human rights, and by speaking out and drawing attention to this Vidhu created the momentum needed to bring about the necessary change in India. In other words, Vidhu's reason for speaking was clear and grounded. Her setting was warm and inviting. She was able to clearly articulate how Change.org gathers signatures and supports the process of taking a petition to lawmakers. This gave the audience confidence that the platform works and a clear reason to provide their support. They were ready for her ask.

When audiences attend a fundraiser, they are typically open to the idea of participation on a financial level, and they want to hear what is being said. They are choosing to be there. They simply need the opportunity and trust in where they place their support. If you are a non-profit speaker, think of your audience as friends. They want you to succeed, not just for you but for everyone.

At the same time, remember that audience members are varied and may participate in many different ways. Some may share your message or decide to volunteer. Many may offer financial support. Others may challenge you, which may serve to further define your message and your methods.

CAMPAIGNING AND RALLIES

A politician or activist needs to face front at all times when on stage. They must speak directly to the audience. Their mindset is that their facts are correct, and their job is not only to convince the audience that they are right but also to inspire the audience to donate, vote and become active in some way that furthers their cause. A rally is the only place a public speaker can get away with being slightly narcissistic. They can make their speech about themselves, and enjoy the attention, if they have an audience that is there for them. They can also raise their voice. This is unlike all other forms of public speaking, though, and even here the focus on yourself should be rare and not too loud. This is where a speaker needs to strike a balance between passion and pushiness.

There are many politicians and activists who are great speakers, and from recent times I'd have to put Bill Clinton at the top of this list. For over 30 years, Clinton has been consistently delivering strong speeches. There might be a speech here or there that ranks higher than his on polls, but no one else has had the consistency he has had in delivering successful speeches. He must absolutely love public speaking, because when a speaker enjoys this art, the audience enjoys watching them.

PANEL DISCUSSIONS

When you've been asked to speak on a panel (because you are an expert in the field), the audience is there to learn from your personal or professional journey, your successes and your mistakes.

To prepare, start with this mindset. Next, write out your introduction. Depending on the type of panel discussion it is, you will have one to two minutes to introduce yourself, your background and what you are currently working on. Some moderators will give you questions ahead of time and you can prepare your answers to these before the session.

However, if the session is one that is open to the audience, you will not have time to prepare for every possible question the audience may ask. My advice is to write down a series of questions (five to seven) you may be asked given the topic and audience. You do not have to memorize answers. Writing the questions down will help you to bullet-point your thoughts. The best type of delivery on a panel is slow, warm and to the point. Less is more. There is often a lot to absorb in a short time. Do the audience a favour and be concise.

If the audience is looking to you for advice, try to leave them with a final statement of encouragement. I once coached an angel investor who wanted to leave an audience of founders with a statement regarding the realities of Silicon Valley start-ups. We decided on "It will be tough, you will have set-backs, but don't give up, keep pushing until you hit the right idea." A combination of reality and encouragement is a great way to end on a panel.

PERSONAL SETTINGS

It's incredibly endearing to see a confident, successful entrepreneur turn to mush when faced with giving a toast at a wedding, a graduation or another personal event.

If you are asked to give (or put in the position of giving) a speech or toast and you feel unusually nervous, know that this is quite common. You are not alone. Firstly, it's outside most people's comfort zone to speak about their loved ones in public. Secondly, if you've been speaking in public confidently for a while, you probably have a system in place for delivery. Now, that system is being disrupted. You are not arguing a case, discussing your business or delivering data. You are speaking from a personal place where exposing some degree of feeling is required. That alone can make a seasoned speaker nervous and hesitant. There is nothing to hide behind, and chances are you might get slightly emotional.

In order to get through this experience and perhaps even enjoy it, you must breathe through it. Use the breath exercises in Part Two to warm up, and breathe slowly throughout your speech. Check in with your mindset. In other words, remind yourself that, while it might feel like all eyes are on you, the truth is that everyone is there to see the bride and groom, the person whose birthday it is, or the casket. You are simply speaking at a heightened personal event. Take your focus off yourself and onto the centre of the event, which is your reason for being there.

WHEN YOU'VE CHOSEN THE WRONG SETTING

On one occasion, I failed to recognize when my style of speaking did not lend to an effective delivery for a given audience. I had been asked to speak at a political rally. Even with ten years of acting training and two voice and speech pedagogical degrees, I came across as nervous and wanting to hide.

This is not surprising in retrospect. I am a natural introvert. I love acting and teaching, but I do not like being the centre of attention. As an actress, I was able to be on stage and be seen playing a part. Delivering well-written words and serving a playwright's intention are vastly different from being yourself in front of a group of people. As for teaching, I am never nervous, as it's the students that matter to me. I want them to walk away remembering what they learned; whether they remember me at all is not important.

When I saw the footage of the rally, I immediately recognized that my style is not well suited to that kind of setting. Nor is presenting at rallies something I want to do – and it showed! I do not want to tell others what to think, feel or do. This was an excellent professional and personal lesson for me.

If you find yourself in a situation that isn't right for you, you can always adjust. Ask yourself what is required for this particular setting and how you can rise to the occasion. You can also consider not taking the opportunity and letting a better fit take your place.

IF YOU ARE STRUGGLING
TO FIND PURPOSE

If you are struggling to find your purpose, or to connect with the theme of your speech, instead of forcing it or being discouraged, ask yourself why. Why am I feeling stuck or hesitant? What's in the way? Do I feel like a fraud? Do I feel that I am not enough of an expert? That I am miscast for the speech? Do I belong?

See where these questions lead and investigate the feelings you are having about the speech and the setting. This may take you into challenges addressed in Part One of this book. If so, refer back to the mindsets discussed in those chapters and the exercises provided. Through this investigation, you may also have many insights that fuel the content of your speech.

In addition, consider your relationship with the audience. Look for any judgments you may be carrying. Are you assuming or concerned that they are not going to understand your material? Or that your speech is a lost cause? That no one cares or that no one is going to believe you?

You need to go from judging the situation to assessing it. How can you turn a perceived lack of understanding or hostility into an opportunity? How can you make your material more relatable?

Again, what can you control and what can you not? What do you know about the audience? What are you assuming that you actually do not know?

For instance, a chief technology officer (CTO) may assume that no one will understand the engineering behind a project. The CTO needs to adapt and get creative in order to match the content and purpose with the environment. The audience may not know the technical jargon or hard science, but is it possible to present the material in a way that is accessible? Don't sell yourself or your audience short by making assumptions when what you need is creative thinking.

FORWARD MOTION

The key is to realize the importance of identifying and grounding yourself in the key purposes and objectives of your speech. Grounding in this purpose takes the focus and pressure off yourself and the things you cannot control. This will help you to focus on your content and free you up to give a more powerful delivery.

As you develop this skill and practice, listen to speeches. Listen for the purposes embedded in the content. Take time to analyse specific speeches that interest you and to look underneath for the purpose that shapes the content being shared. You can also bring this approach into your daily life by simply becoming aware of the intentions that drive your actions. With awareness, you can fine-tune or greatly reconsider your intentions – even, in many cases, without changing the action itself. Simple daily actions may either reveal or be newly filled with intent.

10.
Structure And Storytelling

———

Know Your Content,
Tell a Story

———

> *"People think that stories are shaped by people.*
> *In fact it's the other way around."*
> Terry Pratchett, *Witches Abroad*

Humans are born storytellers. We are hardwired to share experience and information, and to connect with each other using stories.

Stories are a powerful tool for sharing information. They can take an audience from point A to point B experientially, not just intellectually. Stories reflect life and how we perceive. They distil experiences very quickly and colourfully. Stories pull the audience in. Most involve a setting, characters, action, a conflict and a resolution. They make your content relatable and memorable. They tap into the audience's imagination, making them more present through vivid images and feelings.

Stories help the audience connect with the speaker and build a rapport so the audience is more open to suggestion. Most audiences are predisposed to be sceptical about what the speaker is saying, unless they know them well or have been following them through media outlets. They may be wondering, "What is this person really going to teach me about life?" This scepticism is a part of our culture. By telling a story, by getting people to relax and relate, you start to open their minds to different ideas.

Stories seduce your audience into engaging with whatever you are sharing. Sometimes stories can lower the reservations of the audience and make it easier for them to experience different emotions throughout the rest of the speech. But the challenge with storytelling is that in public view or on stage we tend to feel intimidated, or fear that we are not good at storytelling, or that others won't like what we have to say.

In this chapter, we explore how storytelling informs and enriches the structure, content and message of your presentations. Then, we get into the nitty-gritty of what makes a story and storytelling come alive on stage.

STRUCTURE

Your speech is in itself a kind of story. You are taking the audience on a journey from the speech's beginning through to the end. In the beginning, you introduce what the speech is about – why you are giving the speech. You set the stage. What is the challenge that the audience faces? In the middle, you develop the important themes and share the material that supports your message. The end brings everything together, summarizes the content and often gives a call to action to the audience.

Playwrights, screenwriters, scriptwriters, cultural anthropologists, bards and poets have analysed, explored, and stretched story and speech structure for centuries. In *Resonate*, Nancy Duarte finds a 'Hero's Journey' structure at the heart of many great speeches, where the audience is the hero and the speaker is the mentor. Duarte analyses what makes a good story:

*Let's remember that there is one indisputable attribute of a good story: There must be some kind of conflict or imbalance perceived by the audience that your presentation resolves. This sense of discord is what persuades them to care enough to jump in. In a presentation, you create imbalance by consciously juxtaposing **what is** with **what could be**.*

*Clearly contrast who the audience is when they walk into the room (in their ordinary world) with whom they could be when they leave the room (crossing the threshold into a special world). **What is** versus **what could be**. Drawing attention to that gap forces the audience to contend with the imbalance until a new balance is achieved.*

Two clear turning points in a presentation's structure guide the audience through the content and distinctively separates the beginning from the middle and the middle from the end. The first is the call to adventure – this should show the audience a gap between what is and what could be – jolting the audience from complacency.

When effectively constructed – an imbalance is created – the audience will want your presentation to resolve this imbalance. The second turning point is the call to action, which identifies what the audience needs to do or how they need to change. This second turning point signifies that you're coming to the presentation's conclusion.[1]

Resonate is a fascinating book that will help you explore your understanding of story structure. The main point is to move between 'what is' and 'what could be' as you develop your message. By doing so, you will provide the audience with a forward motion that engages them in a discovery process since there is something at stake for them and the world.

Remember that, although storytelling is hardwired in all of us, we have the capacity to develop this skill. But, at the same time, we don't have to invent a structure. Duarte finds these elements to be present consciously and unconsciously in great speeches because it's how our minds work, and how we've been listening and telling stories for centuries. If you consider what you want to say and why, and relate it to the audience in front of you, you will most likely present in a similar fashion.

GENRES

The theme and purpose of your speech open the door to all that you will include in it. What kind of speech are you giving? What are you going to talk about? What information is going to make your points?

There are as many genres of speech as there are kinds of film or book: lectures, addresses, toasts, eulogies, sales pitches, personal stories, political speeches, art presentations and so forth. We explored some of these in Chapter 9, on purpose. Here, we return to TED Talks and use them as an example of a modern-day public laboratory of storytelling and speechmaking.

There are basically five types of TED Talk, and these can be used as training examples for effective speechmaking. Consider as you read what you really want to do with your audience and what the best formula may be.

I believe the speeches listed below strongly represent their genres and use them well.[2] However, this is, of course, subjective. You may find other examples that better appeal to you and inspire your creative process.

1. **Explaining**: Simon Sinek, 2009 "How Great Leaders Inspire Action"
2. **Personal Journey**: Ben Davis, 2014 "The Bay Lights"
3. **Discovery**: Jill Bolte Taylor, 2008 "My Stroke of Insight"
4. **History**: Joshua Prager, 2015 "Wisdom from Great Writers on Every Year of Life"
5. **Challenging**: Bryan Stevenson, 2012 "We Need to Talk about an Injustice"

EXPLAINING
Simon Sinek, "How Great Leaders Inspire Action"

With this style, you explain something that seems phenomenal or mysterious, and simplify it for the audience. Simon Sinek explains how Apple's "Think Different" campaign (used between 1997 and 2002) was part of why Apple became the most profitable company in the world. He compares TIVO's and Apple's marketing strategies to show that people buy products based on why they are made. Apple sold its product by linking it to identity and lifestyle, and what it meant to the people who used it. Apple appealed to people who challenged

---

1 Nancy Duarte, *Resonate* (USA, John Wiley and Sons, 2010), pp. 34 and 36.
2 These speeches can all be accessed at www.ted.com/talks.

the status quo and who led others. By revealing this marketing process, Sinek shows a way of looking at marketing, but he also reveals how people relate to products, and how products connect to what motivates people and their sense of belonging. He opens people's awareness to something that is simple and right, and in front of them, yet often hidden.

PERSONAL JOURNEY
Ben Davis, "The Bay Lights"

In this talk, Ben Davis explains how he came up with the idea to put lights on San Francisco's Bay Bridge, how he got the funding and why he did it. While drinking a cup of coffee staring at the Bay Bridge, which has been eclipsed by the Golden Gate Bridge since it was built, it occurred to him that a light display along the side of the bridge would beautify the entire area. After he initially dismissed the idea as 'silly', he realized his decision-making had always been motivated by love or fear. He made the decision, as he sat with his coffee, to never choose the latter again. Davis describes, step by step, how he made the decision. He attempts to inspire the audience, through his personal narrative, to let go of fear as a factor in their decision-making.

Davis reveals how he struggled with his own inner dialogue. This is intimate and relatable. Many clients have told me how they face such a terrible inner critic or how they are afraid to fail. When someone stands on stage and is willing to expose who they are on the inside, people respond. Davis is also generous with details that describe the environment. He lets his imagination guide us into the world with him. We live through his personal journey until he poses the question to the audience that he also posed to himself: Are you going to choose to make your decisions from a place of love or from fear? His journey prepares us to make the journey ourselves.

DISCOVERY

Jill Bolte Taylor, "My Stroke of Insight"

This genre is similar to the personal journey. In this speech, Jill Bolte Taylor describes her stroke, the altered physical state she entered and the profound discoveries she made while in recovery. Based on those discoveries, she decided to step into the place of peace she experienced near death. Bolte Taylor encourages the audience to explore the differences between right- and left-brain thinking, and to choose to live and project peace. She allows herself to be completely emotionally available to the audience in a generous way. Her courage, availability and expansiveness allow her to paint and transmit to the audience the picture and feeling of what peace would do for the world. The defining aspect of the discovery story is courage. You need to allow yourself the same courageousness as Bolte Taylor in order to tell a story that no one else has told before or in a way no one has told it.

HISTORY

Joshua Prager, "Wisdom from Great Writers on Every Year of Life"

Joshua Prager gives a moving talk about the stages of life and the human condition by analysing authors and the content of well-known books. According to Prager, books are representative of our past, present and future.

This speech centres on learning from the past, and how public speakers can use examples from the past to make a point or to support ideas in a way that will be interesting for the audience. Prager shares what books teach us about human existence. The human emotions of greed, power, lust and love have been with us since the beginning. All you need to do is read about them.

Lessons from the past may also be used to present how the future could take shape. A key point in this genre is to use examples that the audience already has a connection with.

CHALLENGING
Bryan Stevenson, "We Need to Talk about an Injustice"

This style is one of the trickiest to deliver. As a lawyer representing incarcerated youth, Bryan Stevenson asks the audience to rethink the death penalty. He challenges the audience to question their beliefs and values. This isn't an easy thing to do without alienating those being challenged, especially when the subject encroaches on their sense of identity. Stevenson's warmth and storytelling techniques, however, make this an effective, thought-provoking talk that avoids the pitfall of being preachy.

Stevenson charms the audience to some degree by sharing stories about his childhood that shaped his outlook on life. First you imagine him as a child, then you imagine the children whom he defends. As he talks about the death penalty for children, he brings real experiences into your mind. He is very personal and appeals to the audience's empathy. You get to know him as he shapes your experience of the topic. He builds his credibility. Even if you do not agree with him, you will respect him and think about what he said. He shows, through story, how he arrived at his own experience, and the audience is able to relate to this.

WHAT STORY TO TELL?

You may tell a story that comprises the totality of your speech. More often, you will weave numerous stories into your talk. Out of the many hundreds of stories that Stevenson could have called upon, he chose those that served his message and those that he felt would most connect with his audience.

Sometimes a story you wish to tell immediately leaps into your mind. For other speeches, you may need to take time to consider what will really work for this particular talk, the audience and the current moment.

Tell stories you have a personal connection with or develop a strong familiarity with the ones you choose, as this will enable you to integrate them most naturally into your delivery. If your speech has aspects of a personal journey or discovery, it's best to start with a story that pulls the audience in.

BRAINSTORMING

Choosing your stories is part of the overall creative process of generating your content. There's no one way to arrive at the speech you will give. Expect to write and rewrite as your thoughts and ideas flow forth. Often the best place to start is with a brainstorm. This allows you to freely consider your topic without any pressure to edit or structure your thinking or composition. You can then draw on the brainstorm to outline your speech and enrich it with the best, most relevant content you've gathered.

Brainstorming is an art in and of itself. In general, consider what your speech could include. What are your themes and messages? What has relevance for the audience, for the location, for the moment in time? What questions are you asking? What questions are you answering? What goals do you have? What resistance might the audience or critics have? What are the counterarguments? In short, what are the most important, relevant topics for you to cover? These may form the sections of your speech.

From there, you may want to consider all the supporting material – the data, facts, research, quotes, stories (personal, historical, etc.) and so forth. For each category, let your mind roam. Keep asking: What's important? What's interesting?

Let yourself daydream. Take a walk. Let your intuition lead.

Ask others for their ideas, thoughts and perspectives. Research the topic in books, newspapers, films, blogs or however else you may find insights and information. If you are presenting at a conference or event, ask the curator what interests them about your topic.

While brainstorming, you are not committing to anything, so feel very free to write down anything and everything. Follow your ideas and intuitions wherever they lead. These excursions, however outlandish, may lead to real jewels that reach the heart of your speech or colour it with relevant insight and stories.

INVIGORATE YOUR
STORYTELLING

"The purpose of a storyteller is not to tell you how to think, but to give you questions to think upon."
Brandon Sanderson, *The Way of Kings*

After you've chosen your stories, you need to focus on telling them well. What follows here is a selection of simple techniques – using details, imagery, word stress and delight – to invigorate your stories and your storytelling delivery. You can apply these to any speech, regardless of content or whether you are memorizing it partially (using bullet points) or fully.

Read through the sections that follow on these skills, then practise the exercises and bring them into your own speeches. Practise until it's second nature to apply the principles. You may find your new habits forming in everyday speaking.

All the techniques and exercises in this book are meant to support you. Use the exercises to help you bring out the best in your speech and allow your natural charisma to be revealed. If you feel bogged down by any of them, take a more playful, experimental attitude. Or let them go for now. You can always return to them later.

ADD DETAILS

Details bring your audience into the particular world and moment you are creating. When you tell a story, don't hesitate to zoom in and out of setting and character details. An easy way to start is to set the time and place. Give details of the era, year and month to support the story. What are the physical surroundings? Describe a character or yourself in a way that is relatable. When quoting your characters, use common language that reflects how they would actually speak. Review your speech by asking, where would specific details heighten the experience for the audience?

STORYTELLING REQUIRES IMAGERY

Imagery is a powerful vehicle for bringing an audience to a place. It creates mental images in the audience's minds that connect what you are saying to what they are imagining. Whether you are giving a TED Talk, a conference presentation, a keynote, a pitch or any other kind of speech, use imagery to enliven your delivery by stressing or delivering words with the feeling they conjure.

Robert F. Kennedy's speech the night after Martin Luther King Jr's assasination uses imagery to create a powerful effect. As you read the excerpt, notice how images, even sensations, are strongly conjured in your mind.

EXERCISE 25

WORD STRESS

Duration: 10 minutes

**PURPOSE: INVIGORATE IMAGES
WITHIN YOUR STORY**

**ROBERT F. KENNEDY
REMARKS TO THE CLEVELAND CITY CLUB, 5 APRIL 1968**

How you stress words within your sentences affects both your cadence and the weight the words are given in the minds of your audience. This is another powerful, simple way to bring the audience into what you are saying. Here, we will use an excerpt from Robert F. Kennedy's speech to explore how to stress words and the impact this has.

Step 1: Read the following out loud and record yourself:
This is a time of shame and sorrow. It is not a day for politics. I have saved this one opportunity to speak briefly to you about this mindless menace of violence in America which again stains our land and every one of our lives. It is not the concern of any one race. The victims of the violence are black and white, rich and poor, young and old, famous and unknown. They are, most important of all, human beings whom other human beings loved and needed. No one – no matter where he lives or what he does – can be certain who will suffer from some senseless act of bloodshed.

Step 2: Read only the underlined words out loud (again, recording yourself). Whenever you use this technique, if the story or speech has been well written, you should get the foundation from the stressed words alone.

This is a time of <u>shame</u> and <u>sorrow</u>. It is <u>not</u> a day for <u>politics</u>. I have saved this one opportunity to <u>speak</u> briefly to you about this <u>mindless</u> <u>menace</u> of <u>violence</u> in <u>America</u> which again <u>stains</u> our <u>land</u> and every one of our <u>lives</u>. It is not the concern of any one race. The <u>victims</u> of the <u>violence</u> are <u>black</u> and <u>white</u>, rich and poor, young and old, famous and unknown. They are, most important of all, <u>human beings</u> whom other human beings <u>loved</u> and <u>needed</u>. No one – no matter where he <u>lives</u> or what he does – can be certain who will <u>suffer</u> from some <u>senseless</u> act of <u>bloodshed</u>.

Step 3: Now record yourself reading the full version above with the underlined words stressed. You can stress a word by saying it louder or slower, or over-articulating it. What differences do you notice when you listen and compare the two versions?

FIND DELIGHT

Be delighted by the story you are telling. The basic principle behind method acting is that the audience experiences to some degree what you do.

There's a certain natural delight in storytelling that we often hold back or seem to forget. Find the delight, the enjoyment or the richness in the story you are telling. You can feel this very clearly when Bryan Stevenson talks about his grandmother. His voice and manner shift as if he re-experiences the hugs as he describes them. He appears delighted by the story and so are we.

You can allow yourself, as the speaker, to re-experience the story that you are telling. Let the images come and influence you to feel that you are there. Take the audience there by describing where you are.

Details – even short, specific details – will create a world for the listener and enable you to be present in the moment as well. If you are telling a deeper, personal story, that personal level could make you feel vulnerable.

When you feel your emotions rise, allow them to be there and don't fight the organic process. When you start to tear up or your throat starts to tighten, or if any other physiological response arises from that vulnerability, then connect to your breathing. You can gently and patiently manage your physiological responses. You know you are not going to fall because you have technique and a blueprint to support you. You are grounded in your story and your purpose. You can address your fears through your commitment.

MEMORIZE OR BULLET POINT?

To memorize or not to memorize? The short answer is, it depends. You may or may not want to memorize, depending on the length of the speech, the purpose, the setting and how you work best. If it's a TED Talk, yes. For the TED speaker, the guidelines of the conference are rigid. A curator has to see and approve of your content after which you do not want to deviate from it. One of the advantages of memorizing your speech is that it gives you a chance to explore and review the content very deeply. You may make micro-edits to improve the text or to find a rhythm that makes it a better story.

If you are giving a short speech that is timed, memorizing is best. Short speeches need to be concise. Don't cheat yourself by thinking you can bullet-point a five-minute speech. Doing this will likely cause you to forget a valuable point or message, and you'll find yourself regretting it. If you are nervous and worried that you will forget content by using bullet points, then memorize – you are doing something to support yourself.

At conferences where you are delivering a lot of technical information, you are better off bullet-pointing your thoughts and then being more spontaneous. Really technical information is a bit more difficult to memorize, and you will likely need to use slides to keep you on track.

If your speech is about a product that you have built, it is likely that you'll know your material very well and not need to write down or memorize your speech.

Ultimately, if you have the choice, whether to memorize or not depends on how *you* work best. Having said that, try not to box yourself in by memorizing word for word. Your speech should be malleable to make room for new thoughts, responding to the audience, and technical difficulties or unplanned moments you can take advantage of.

EXERCISE 26
MEMORIZATION MOMENT TO MOMENT
Duration: Depends on speech length

PURPOSE: BE CONFIDENT AND
PRESENT DURING YOUR SPEECH

This memorization technique, based on a method used by many actors, uses logic and imagery to link together the moments in your speech in order to help you better remember and understand why you are where you are in the text. If you get into the logical structure of the speech and find the flow of images that connect one section to the next, your recall will come naturally.

STEP 1
After you've written your speech, go through the text moment to moment and ask yourself "Why?". Why are you saying this at this particular moment? Label your reason for speaking. Here is an example based on the structure of a typical speech:

Introduction: I'm introducing myself, my company, a problem, a takeaway or a new idea.
Support: I'm supporting my introduction with data, credentials and history.
Memories: I'm storytelling with detailed descriptions. I'm visualizing all the elements of the story that I've lived through or recounting something someone else lived through.
Put it together: What does it all mean? Here, I am linking all previous thoughts.

Takeaway (usually this is at the end of your speech – however, you could have a few takeaways within the speech as well):

Specific example: Excerpt from Steve Jobs' 2005 Stanford Commencement Speech.

Memories: Woz and I started Apple in my parents' garage when I was 20. We worked hard, and in ten years Apple had grown from just the two of us in a garage into a two-billion-dollar company with over 4,000 employees. We released our finest creation – the Macintosh, a year earlier – and I had just turned 30.

Introduction takeaway: And then I got fired. How can you get fired from a company you started?

Support of introduction takeaway: Well, as Apple grew we hired someone who I thought was very talented to run the company with me, and for the first year or so things went well. But then our visions of the future began to diverge and eventually we had a falling out. When we did, our board of directors sided with him. So, at 30, I was out. And very publicly out.

Put it together: What had been the focus of my entire adult life was gone, and it was devastating.

Takeaway: I didn't see it then, but it turned out that getting fired from Apple was the best thing that could have ever happened to me. The heaviness of being successful was replaced by the lightness of being a beginner again, less sure about everything. It freed me to enter one of the most creative periods of my life.

STEP 2

After you've labelled the sections of your speech, read it out loud. Put the text down and recite it. If you forget what's next, ask yourself, what was the previous moment? Was it an introduction you need to support? Or a support you need to tie together? A takeaway and now you are on a new section?

Only look at the text after you've asked several questions. If you continually look at the text without thinking through the structure, you will become dependent on seeing the words. Resist the urge! You'll gradually internalize the structure and this will be the foundation of your recall.

If you find you are continually forgetting the same part of the speech each time you rehearse it, ask yourself "Why?". There is likely a reason. Once you've determined why you are forgetting it, you can decide to either back it up with more commitment or cut the section.

Speakers will forget the line that they do not feel comfortable with or that may not be necessary. You may not even notice you are leaving the line out. Record yourself once you think you have the speech memorized. Some possible reasons for leaving lines and words out could include:

- You are not committed to expressing that particular idea.
- It is not part of the storytelling you are visualizing.
- You added in a joke or something that "sounded good", but in reality it does not add anything.

BULLET POINTING

When bullet pointing your sections and talking points, think about what your objective is and what tone you want to match with the objective. I will talk more about this in Chapter 11, on pausing and pacing.

Use a method similar to memorizing to ensure a solid bullet point foundation. Ask yourself: Why does this point or section follow the previous point? What's its purpose? What's the end or resolution? Make changes to reflect stronger connectivity. This causality within the flow will not only help you recall what you want to say but also make natural, logical sense to the audience.

If someone is not memorizing their speeches but is having a lot of issues with delivery, I ask them to write their speeches down. This allows them to see what they are actually saying compared to what they want to say. They may be struggling with how they structure their talk, and not making strong, logical connections between their points.

Strong storytelling creates memorable speeches. In the next chapter, we delve deeper into delivery skills that strengthen your presence and that you can rely on no matter the content or circumstances of your presentations.

11.
Tone, Pacing, Pausing And Body Language

———

Matching Delivery
and Content

———

"Suit the action to the word, the word to the action,
with this special observance: that you o'erstep
not the modesty of nature."
Shakespeare, *Hamlet*

In 2007, I was waiting in a classroom with 17 others for my first day of teacher training with Cicely Berry. Ms Berry, well into her 80s, was undoubtedly the most successful and famous Shakespearean acting coach alive. She was the voice, speech and text director of the Royal Shakespeare Company (RSC) for 40 years, and is credited with the success of the RSC as much as the artistic directors.

When Ms Berry entered the room, she had a cane in one hand and a stack of scripts in the other. She walked slowly to a chair set for her at the front of the room and mindfully sat down. Without a word or another gesture, she threw the scripts out across the room. They scattered and came to a full stop. The 18 of us froze. We looked at the scripts, then looked back at her.

She appeared infuriated. Then, she stood, suddenly, and shouted, "Pick up those scripts! If you can't get up and pick scripts off the floor, you can't speak Shakespeare ... Now get up!"

We immediately went into action, each of us making a beeline for the nearest script. Our training with Ms Berry had begun, and it was rigorous. Performing in a Shakespeare play demands the full use of your body, mind and emotional life. We matched our movements, emotions and articulation to imagery and punctuation, until our characters came fully alive in our interactions.

In this chapter, we explore essential techniques for developing a delivery that matches your content and that brings your message to life in a way that ensures you reach your audience. While we will not be delivering Shakespeare, we will enter the heart of the training for vibrant use of language and gesture. Practise until these skills are second nature, and you will be able to rely on your technique, not circumstance or guesswork.

TONE

Christopher, a chief financial officer at a local tech company, came to my studio concerned that he was not developing a rapport with his board of directors. Responsible for delivering quarterly reports, he entered every presentation feeling intimidated and left feeling cold. This was despite the fact that the reports had been positive every quarter he'd worked at the company.

The first thing I asked Christopher to do in the studio was to deliver a report so I could see what he was doing. At the end, I had to ask him whether he was delivering good news or whether he was announcing that the *Titanic* was sinking. His tone was dour; it was more suitable for a eulogy than for sharing the successes of a company strategy that he'd been stewarding day in and day out.

I suggested to Christopher that he match his content with his delivery. When he didn't understand what this meant, I recorded him as he repeated his speech. This time, when he observed the playback, he burst out laughing: "It looks like I'm saying that someone has died."

From there, I asked him to pick different emotions that matched the reports and to experiment with communicating those emotions. He explored confidence and pride, happiness and a sense of encouragement. The difference was palpable – here was an executive who was on top of his job and engaged with the information he had to share.

Once Christopher felt the naturalness of matching his delivery with the content, he also realized his sombreness was a reaction to his fear of the board. He told me that, "The whole tone was like a wall put up to block the intimidation I felt."

This is not unusual when we speak to those with authority. Sometimes it is self-imposed – in other words, the authority figures are not judging us at all. We project our own fears and wall ourselves off. Other times, the authority figures, the board of directors in this case, may be judgmental, cold or downright hostile.

Nonetheless, in either situation basic logic dictates that sharing great news should be happy and upbeat. You are positive about it, or proud and sincere, or at the very least neutral and not depressive. If you are sharing a discovery, success or a win of any kind, the audience will only be moved and excited if you are. All audiences experience, to some degree, the experience of the speaker.

Sharing negative information, meanwhile, is often harder for people because they do not want to come across as false, or they are not clear about what level of responsibility they have for the information they share. In Christopher's case, if he had negative news, he would need to communicate in a serious, sincere tone that he was taking responsibility and actively involved in working to improve the situation.

If your audience really is hostile, ground yourself in the truth, or what you believe to be the truth, and how it may benefit others. In other words, they may not want to hear you, and they may not agree with you, but there is an opportunity here for some of the people in your audience to look at your topic through a new perspective. Bring courage, fortitude, creativity and respect into your tone – rather than fear, judgment or discouragement.

Every situation will have its own nuances. The main point here is that we need to train ourselves to clarify our emotional experience while we access a broader emotional palette (a wide range of appropriate emotions) that matches our content. This conveys presence, responsibility and relatability to your audience.

EXERCISE 27
MATCHING TONE TO CONTENT
IN SECTIONS OF A SPEECH
Duration: 30 minutes

PURPOSE: CREATE A SINCERE CONNECTION
TO YOUR TEXT AND AUDIENCE

In Chapters 9 and 10, we explored grounding your speech in your content and your purpose. Here you are taking the next step of matching your delivery and tone to the feeling of the content as it changes in different parts of your speech. You may already be doing this unconsciously to one degree or another, as it's natural for us to imbue our language with our emotions. The goal here is to make this explicit – to make matching our tone and our content a principle of our delivery.

Use this exercise to clarify the tone of your content and to identify any confusion or places where you may be holding back the feeling that most supports your message.

Step 1: Select a speech you are working on or another speech of your own or someone else that you can practise with.

Step 2: Separate your speech into sections.

Step 3: Mark the speech with the objective, content and suitable delivery style for each section.

Step 4: Record yourself as you deliver your speech, notice whether you naturally shift your tone.

Step 5: Observe the areas where your tone is not clear or naturally matching your intentions. Practise these areas until the shifts are fluid and natural.

Here is a sample template for a four-part speech for a business conference or pitch:

PART OF SPEECH: INTRODUCTION

Objective: Clearly articulate who you are and what your company does.

Delivery that is suitable: A tone that is warm, upbeat, excited or welcoming. These are not the only choices, but they are often appropriate for conferences.

PART OF SPEECH: PROBLEM

Objective: Describe, in detail, the challenge that your company is working on to address customer demands. Make it relatable.

Delivery that is suitable: Concern, hyper-focused, astonished, perhaps a sense of urgency to change the current conditions.

PART OF SPEECH: SOLUTION

Objective: Define research and development, establish credibility and earn trust.

Delivery that is suitable: Proud, upbeat, lighter than the problem section. The solution should always have a different tone from the problem. To me, this is basic logic. However, when we are stressed and pressured, sometimes we forget basic logic. Public speaking is dynamic when we keep things simple.

PART OF SPEECH: SUMMARY

Objective: Share how the audience can use the information.

Delivery that is suitable: Warm, approachable, inviting.

PACING

Along with your tone, your pacing has a powerful impact on your audience. Many speakers, especially those new to audiences, will speed up the rate of their speech when they present. This may be due to adrenaline or nerves, a sense of pressure to explain too much in a short amount of time, or pressure to 'entertain' coupled with a fear of being boring. If you have this habit, but these reasons do not fit you, examine some other possibilities. Why might you speed up unnecessarily?

In general, a minimum baseline for your speed is to never speak faster than your articulators can shape sound. The audience needs to understand you. You mustn't speak so fast that your speech becomes mumbled. If you have the habit of a fast pace while speaking, slowing down will likely feel abnormally slow – even painfully slow. Lean towards speaking slower than what feels right or normal. Eventually you may enjoy the spaciousness that this brings to your experience.

EXERCISE 28
SLOWING YOUR PACE
Duration: 10 minutes

PURPOSE: ALLOW YOUR AUDIENCE
TO DIGEST WHAT YOU ARE SAYING

Step 1: Read through this short excerpt from Franklin D. Roosevelt's Inaugural Address from 1933:

So, first of all, let me assert my firm belief that the only thing we have to fear is fear itself – nameless, unreasoning, unjustified terror which paralyzes needed efforts to convert retreat into advance. In every dark hour of our national life, a leadership of frankness and of vigor has met with that understanding and support of the people themselves, which is essential to victory. And I am convinced that you will again give that support to leadership in these critical days.

Step 2: Record yourself speaking the speech out loud.

Step 3: Do Exercise 15 (in Part Two) to assist in slowing your delivery down.

Step 4: Record yourself again, consciously slowing your speed down. You may speed up in certain areas, but for the most part you should aim to speak more slowly than you would normally do in front of an audience.

Step 5: Listen to the first recording, then the second. Note the differences.

I've chosen this particular Roosevelt speech because it is a great example of how fast and slow pacing have different effects on an audience. A fast pace could convey a sense of urgency while a slower pace could convey calm reassurance.

MATCHING SPEED TO CONTENT

Using an overall slower pace does not mean you should use the same pace throughout your speech. Once you feel comfortable slowing the overall speed of your speech, practise matching your speed to the content. Think of yourself as a car with a manual transmission. Some thoughts will be in second gear, others in third and occasionally some in fourth. The biggest takeaway, your essential points, should be slow and thoughtful.

If you have been filmed speaking at a conference, or event of any kind, listen to how quickly you are speaking. Look for places within the speech where the message may have been compromised due to speed. Look for natural places to slow down. The first of these should be your introduction of yourself and/or the content. This is your opportunity to create rapport with the audience. Rapport is created with slow, deliberate warmth and thoughtfulness. Other places to slow down are your key messages.

Variation is important. You can speak as slowly as you want as long as you apply an occasional shift into a faster speed with appropriate word stress. A great example of a speaker who could captivate an audience with slow speech but who also understood how to shift into faster speeds was Barbara Jordan. I highly recommend watching Jordan deliver her 1976 Democratic National Committee (DNC) Keynote Address. You could listen to any of her speeches, but there's something especially thoughtful about her pacing in this speech, in which she was the first African American woman to give a DNC keynote.

PAUSING

"The music is not in the notes, but in the silence between."
Commonly attributed to Wolfgang Amadeus Mozart

Humans are not built to constantly hear and take in information. Continuously listening to the sound of a human speaking, especially while being expected to remember facts, ideas or discussions is exhausting.

There is a need for silence when speaking. If you habitually speed up when giving speeches or presentations, a pause can feel excruciatingly long or even unnecessary because you are not prioritizing your audience's ability to digest what you are saying. My advice, as always, is to record yourself. When you listen back, ask yourself:

* Did I pause?
* Did I breathe?
* Am I speeding through the delivery with no pausing, or am I verbalizing the pause (see below)?

The word 'digest' is important here. When you digest something, you take it with you. You want the audience to remember what you said and how it made them feel long after you stop speaking.

THE DREADED VERBAL PAUSE

Almost every person I've worked with has had a variation of a verbal pause. The most common is "uhm", occasionally there is a "but uhm" and even more rarely there is "uuuuhhh", when someone is really trying to remember what they want to say. Those who do not have this habit typically had it at one point and worked to remove it.

What causes us to say "uhm" in between our thoughts? Often it's an internal pressure to fill the room with sound.

We fear that the audience's mind will drift if we are not holding it hostage with noise. Or we are avoiding how silence creates a space where we must acknowledge the audience. As described in Part One, letting the audience in to see us is a scary proposition. If we can hide our discomfort in any way, we will.

Here, again, we have a need for a release of physical and mental tension. Instead of a verbal pause, we need to breathe. If you breathe, the audience will as well. While allowing your breath to support your voice, you also allow your breath to support your pauses. Let that silence and openness happen.

How long should a pause last? Eventually this will become second nature. In the meantime, think through the logic. We breathe when we need oxygen. Speaking in a formal or semi-formal setting doesn't change that.

STRATEGIC PLACES FOR PAUSES

If you are asking the audience a question, whether they are required to answer or not, always pause before and after the question. The pause before sets them up to think, and the pause after allows them to do the thinking. It's frankly disrespectful to ask a question and answer it immediately, before the audience has had time to process it. If you are doing this, you are talking at the audience, not to them.

Other strategic places to pause include before and/or after a name. When you introduce a colleague or thank someone during a speech, do not just toss their name out. Give the person their due. These pauses are short, polite pauses. For longer pauses, when you really want the audience to think, especially if you are introducing new ideas or ideas the audience may be resistant to, practise slowing down and taking deeper breaths during poignant moments.

Cesar Chavez, co-founder of the United Farm Workers Association in the US, is a great example of a speaker who understood the power of carefully placed pauses. In his speech "Vote with Your Dollar" 1984, his pauses are unusually long, but the audience stays completely engaged. His pauses seem to express his 110% commitment to what he is saying; he is unwavering. The pauses ground his authority and give a weight to his message, along with time for it to sink in. Even if you disagreed with him, it would be hard to walk away from that speech and not to respect him or be swayed to some level by his commitment.

EXERCISES TO HELP YOU ADD APPROPRIATE PAUSES TO YOUR SPEECHES

In the section above on pacing, I recommended that you check out Barbara Jordan's 1976 DNC Keynote Address. Another fantastic aspect of Jordan's speaking was her use of pauses. The use of a pause is important for the delivery of your message. In order for the audience to relax and listen, you must give them time to digest what you've just said before moving on to the next thought. This does not mean you have to create long pauses at the end of every thought. The length of your pauses can vary. But without them the audience will begin to tune you out. This is also the way to work with long sentences that bring together many thoughts and clauses. Break them up with appropriate pauses.

EXERCISE 29
PAUSING
Duration: 10–15 minutes

**PURPOSE: ALLOW YOUR AUDIENCE TIME
TO THINK ABOUT YOUR MESSAGE**

Step 1: Returning to the same text that you used in Exercise 28 (Roosevelt's 1933 Inaugural Address), decide where the natural pauses are, and mark the text accordingly with slash marks. Use one slash (/) for a short pause and two slashes (//) for a longer pause. Here is an example:

So, first of all / let me assert my firm belief // that the only thing we have to fear is fear itself – // nameless, unreasoning, unjustified terror / which paralyzes needed efforts to convert retreat into advance. // In every dark hour of our national life, a leadership of frankness and of vigour has met with that understanding and support of the people themselves // which is essential to victory. // And I am convinced that you will again give that support to leadership in these critical days.

Step 2: Record yourself speaking the text, pausing longer than you typically would in between important messages.

Step 3: Listen to your recording. Note the differences and how you feel listening. Pauses usually convey calm confidence.

EXERCISE 30

PACING AND PAUSING IN
YOUR OWN SPEECH

Duration: Depends on length of speech

**PURPOSE: APPLY DELIVERY TECHNIQUES
DIRECTLY TO YOUR WORK**

Choose a speech you have given or are currently working on. If you do not have one, select a passage from another person's speech. Read through it once, and then follow the steps in Exercises 28 and 29. In summary, first record yourself giving the speech. Then, record yourself consciously slowing down as you read. Notice the differences. Next, mark the text with short (/) and long (//) pause marks. Record yourself reading the text again, pausing for longer than you normally would at the marks. Notice the differences between the three recordings.

COVERING THE ESSENTIAL POINTS
IN THE ALLOTTED TIME

Think about what is more important to you. Is it to say everything you want to say, or is it for the audience to connect with your message and remember the key points?

When you have a set time to deliver your speech, it may be that you become tempted to speed up your delivery to fit everything in. You must resist this urge. This is one of the primary ways to undermine your entire purpose. Speeding disrespects your message and your audience as it ensures they cannot retain what you say, much like speeding in a car ensures you will not see the details of the scenery.

Pacing and pausing are your allies here. They can also help if you have a natural habit of speeding (as touched upon in Chapter 4).

Record and time yourself using appropriate pacing and pausing. If you go over the allotted time, review your speech. Where can you make a point more succinctly? What words, phrases, paragraphs and stories are superfluous? In short, cut the fat. If you are very far over the time limit, reconsider the purpose of your speech (see Chapter 9). What is the essential message? What are the key points? Distil, distil, distil.

With rare exceptions, your allotted time is all you need for the purpose and setting of each speech you give. You need to have some trust that the time you have is enough, and concern yourself with hitting your bullet points well. Curators of conferences and events, in general, know what they are doing. They will lengthen or cut speech times to suit the event. Use your time limit as an opportunity to focus your talk and to plant the most important seeds in your audience's hearts and minds. Focus on the main question: what does the audience need to hear at this particular time and in this particular place?

If, unexpectedly, you have to shorten your remarks at the last moment, re-evaluate. This is rare, but it can and does happen when another speaker goes over their time limit or some other schedule change is required. Accept the situation. Ask yourself again: what are the most important points? You will find you can cut out more than you thought you could. In fact, you may find your speech improves every time you review it in this manner.

As discussed in Chapter 9, pitches may be anywhere from two to four minutes in length, and the speaker is often asking for large sums of money. Consider what your audience needs to hear – facts, opportunity, significance – versus what story you feel you have to tell. Your directness, clarity and respect for the time limit will convey more than extraneous background. The audience can find all that out later. The pitch is a seed of a plant that can grow to have an enormous scope.

Altogether, it is always better to have a few very clear points that will make your audience want to hear more than to exhaust them with everything you could possibly say. This is particularly true in today's communications environment. There is never just one chance for an audience member to connect with you. Trust that, if they are interested, they will find a way.

This is especially true at conferences. You will most likely announce, at the end of your speech, where you will be for the remainder of the conference and how people can get in touch with you. There is no reason to try to tell your whole story in a couple of minutes.

BODY LANGUAGE AND
STAGE DIRECTION

"Your body communicates as well as your mouth.
Don't contradict yourself."
Allen Ruddock

Posture and coordination are the foundation of body language. When you are neutral and upright with no excess tension or collapse, your voice can function freely and your movements will be grounded and connected. This is your position of power and natural expression.

Some clients ask me what they should do with their hands while speaking. My answer is simply to do what feels natural to you while maintaining a neutral posture. If you have prepared yourself physically with exercises outlined in Part Two, you should not have too much nervous energy. Therefore, you can do whatever you like with your hands – within reason. If it feels natural to gesture occasionally with one or both of your hands, that's fine.

Repetitive gesturing or shaking, however, is the result of excess tension. Excess tension is wasted energy. Take that energy and put it into your vocal delivery. Make your statements deliberate and direct them towards the audience. Remember to breathe and keep your pacing slower than you think it should be. This will mitigate erratic or repetitive gestures.

USING EYE CONTACT TO INVIGORATE YOUR PRESENCE

Many speakers also question where to look while speaking. If you have a large audience (over 100), your eyes should stay at the horizon level, for the most part, as this will connect you with the whole of the audience. If you have a smaller audience you'll need to occasionally make eye contact. Do this with your eyes, not your head. In other words, do not tilt your head down more than necessary. If you have a large audience, or an audience in tiered seating, you'll want to look towards the back rows now and then. The goal is to ensure everyone feels included in your speech by using your eyes.

Even with this instruction, it is common to feel an urge to avoid making eye contact or to move your gaze from the horizon level. You may feel particularly vulnerable or nervous for one reason or another. Pulling your gaze away may seem like a conscious or unconscious way to ground yourself or to escape that feeling of vulnerability.

Whatever the case may be, it also disconnects you from your audience. You are subtly, or not so subtly, communicating that you wish the audience were not there. Avoiding reality will only make your speech miss its mark. Instead, you can choose to fully commit to your content, your purpose and your audience. You can recommit to the reality of the situation.

If you feel yourself wanting to avoid making eye contact, acknowledge that feeling and use it as a reminder to make eye contact. Practising helps. Not only will you grow more accustomed to the feelings that come up in various speaking situations but you will also find that making eye contact becomes very natural and is actually another way to ground yourself.

HOT SPOTS AND CHEATING OUT

For many speeches you will be, more or less, stationary. You may be behind a podium or seated in a chair. If you plan to walk around while you speak, make sure you spend some time on the stage in advance of your talk. Get familiar with the hotspots – the lighted areas of the stage. Stay within those hotspots. Staying in this zone ensures you will be well lit and the audience will not lose connection with you in the shadows.

One of the cardinal rules of theatre acting – and public speaking – is to always cheat out. This means that you always have the front of your body facing the audience. In a play, characters who are not the main focus, and who do not have dialogue, may turn from the audience, coming and going from the stage. But the central actors and the public speaker, which are the main focus, will always cheat out. This simply and directly communicates that you are open and available to the audience. Likewise, the audience will feel they are important to the lead actor or speaker – you. This shows that you are not going away from them or disconnecting.

When there is something behind you that you want to reference or access – a slide or a prop – maintain the forward orientation of your body as you gesture or act. If you take a sip of water or use a prop, do not disconnect. Continue talking and engaging with the audience. Don't ever let them see the back of your head.

KEEPING YOUR SPEECH VITAL

People often marvel that theatre actors can play the same material over and over, often six nights a week, for months. The real marvel is that the performance can stay fresh and vibrant, often improving as time goes by. This is partly due to improved teamwork and familiarity, but it also reveals an ongoing renewal of the cast's commitment to the creative vision and objectives of the play.

Feeling alive and invigorated will likely not be a problem if you deliver your speech once or a few times. However, if you are presenting the same speech many times over many months, it can start to feel stale. How do you keep it fresh?

One way is to switch up some of the content – to access the creative side of your work. Are there different stories you can tell to enliven the message? Are there other aspects of the topic you can explore or emphasize?

You may also return to the original purpose of the speech. Sometimes, with familiarity, you may disconnect from 'the big whys' that motivated your decisions, visions and actions.

Returning to your purposes can restore your focus and renew your engagement with the material. You can then ground and reground in why you are there at this event and what the audience needs to get from it.

In addition, remember that even if you have presented your material many times, for all or the vast majority of the audience it will be fresh. Speak to the freshness of the audience. Speak as if you are having a conversation with someone who has never heard the material before – which is likely the case. Many teachers who deliver the same subject matter year after year find an ongoing delight in sharing it with new students. Similarly, actors who have a strong sense of engagement with the playwright's objectives find it much more compelling to deliver repeated performances than those who do not.

INTEGRATING DELIVERY SKILL

This chapter has covered some of the essential foundations for clear, impactful delivery. The purpose of training in these skills is to make them second nature, so that you can trust your technique, as well as your content and purpose, rather than stressing or guessing. It's similar to the reason why athletes practise their form over and over as they shoot hoops, run or swim. Good form – good technique – is the vehicle. Content and purpose are the fuel. Presence is everything altogether.

The practice, now, is to bring these elements together in your delivery. You can rehearse privately in your own studio, with guest audiences (often family, friends and colleagues) or casually in your daily interactions.

EXERCISE 31
INTEGRATING DELIVERY TECHNIQUES
IN A FORMAL SPEECH
Duration: 10 minutes

**PURPOSE: PRACTICE YOUR EMOTIONAL
CONNECTION TO A TEXT**

Return to Roosevelt's speech (reproduced again below). Read through it briefly and silently, and recall the content and purpose of the speech. Use Exercise 29 to create structure first. Connect with the tone that is appropriate for the speech. Roosevelt is being inaugurated for the first time. The USA was in the midst of the Great Depression. Here he promises renewed prosperity. He embarks on an enormous undertaking that will require not only great effort but also great sacrifice and great resolve. What tone is appropriate for such a speech?

So, first of all, let me assert my firm belief that the only thing we have to fear is fear itself – nameless, unreasoning, unjustified terror which paralyzes needed efforts to convert retreat into advance. In every dark hour of our national life, a leadership of frankness and of vigour has met with that understanding and support of the people themselves, which is essential to victory. And I am convinced that you will again give that support to leadership in these critical days.

I perceive the appropriate tone here to be any combination of serious, grave, resolute, courageous, grounded, energetic and compassionate. These are not easy qualities to express, yet connection with any one of them will help to bring the others forward.

Once you have experienced elements of this tone, speak the speech aloud. Explore the various colours and emphasize the tone as you read the words. Now consider your pacing and pauses. Try to slow down, perhaps more than you initially feel comfortable with. If you have a podium or something that can serve as one, stand at it as you deliver the short excerpt again. If not, sit upright in your chair. Find your position of power – find the open grounding of neutral – and let your breath settle, deepen and engage more fully. Run through the breath warm-ups (Exercises 14 and 15) and the resonance exercises (Exercises 18–20).

Now return to the speech. Imagine that there is an audience in front of you. Let your gaze extend out, make eye contact and take in the entire scene. Now speak aloud to this audience with the appropriate tone, pacing and pausing for what you have to say.

EXERCISE 32
DELIVERY IN DAILY LIFE
Duration: As long as you'd like

PURPOSE: BECOME MORE IMPACTFUL IN MEETINGS, NEGOTIATIONS AND SOCIAL SITUATIONS

Pacing, pausing and eye contact are both extraordinary and very ordinary practices to bring into everyday life. We do not, of course, aim to turn all our conversations into speeches!

Daily life integration, rather, is about bringing more awareness to your habits. Think about the following questions:

- Are you being understood?
- Are you doing a lot of explaining and elaborating, or are you getting straight to the essentials?
- What tone are you using in any particular conversation?
- What tone might better match what you have to say?
- Do you find yourself speaking faster to certain people or in certain situations?
- What happens when you slow down?
- What happens when you pause?
- What happens when your breathing becomes a priority?

Explore pacing, pausing and using more eye contact as you go about your interactions – from ordering a coffee at a cafe to having a meeting with a colleague. Notice your habits and reactions. Notice how these impact your interactions. Your eyes have many expressive qualities you can explore and adjust as well. You may find more space for listening to others, and you may become more aware of your emotional disposition and, therefore, be able to choose more clearly how you want to respond rather than react.

Above all, be patient and gentle with yourself – this is no excuse for judging yourself – and enjoy the process. As you build these habits – of mindfulness and delivery – in your daily life, they will come more naturally and easily on stage without particular effort. You will find you can rely on the techniques you've integrated, regardless of the circumstances you find yourself in. You will speak at various appropriate speeds, pause in strategic places and direct your eye contact naturally to increase connection and the impact of your message.

12.
Presence

———

Being a Leader and
Motivating Others

———

*"There is a vitality, a life force, an energy, a quickening
that is translated through you into action, and because
there is only one of you in all time, this expression is
unique. And if you block it, it will never exist through
any other medium and will be lost."*
Martha Graham, quoted in Agnes de Mille,
The Life and Work of Martha Graham

Presence refers to the command of attention the speaker has from the audience. Presence can be hard to define at times, but you know it when you see it. You feel compelled to listen and watch the speaker. You don't have to like the person, but something pulls you in. Every speaker has a degree of presence. Just by entering the room, you change the landscape.

Within a speaker's presence, there's often a quality of confidence, an awareness that the person can do what they are there to do. A good example of this is Oprah Winfrey. No matter where she is, be it her own show, as a guest speaker or accepting an award, her presence fills the room and extends to those watching from afar. She is confident without bluster, fully present in every moment and extremely professional. On top of all of this, she is modest and can laugh at herself. Audiences love her for it.

The quality of your presence, or your effect on others, is something that can be consciously developed. This chapter focuses on the qualities of speakers who have a strong presence and an essential ingredient they all share: the ability to listen.

CHARISMA AND GRAVITAS

Some believe that charisma or charm is required to have a strong presence on stage or in discussions. That attractiveness that makes you listen is certainly a quality many of the speakers who deliver great speeches possess. They lead us, and we want to follow them.

Yet, I do not believe you need to be charming on stage, at the podium or in a meeting for your presence to be strong and commanding. Charm, rather, is a choice the speaker makes that must be natural to them – even if it is developed through practice.

President John F. Kennedy and his brother Robert F. Kennedy were extraordinary speakers with strikingly different qualities of presence. In John, audiences saw an extremely charming, witty, attractive speaker who could stir others to new missions and ideas. Robert, meanwhile, had an equally commanding presence without the overt charisma, charm and humour.

What Robert had that made him compelling is what we commonly call gravitas. Gravitas is a solemn or weighted seriousness. Robert had the combination of the Kennedy fearlessness, which allowed him to be vulnerable in front of audiences, a belief in himself, and the belief in the greater good that others admired and trusted. He did not need to be liked by his audience – there were more important matters to deal with – and he never compromised himself by pretending to be someone he wasn't.

Here is an example from a speech Robert gave in 1966 that highlights his fearlessness and belief in the greater good.

Few will have the greatness to bend history itself, but each of us can work to change a small portion of events. It is from numberless diverse acts of courage and belief that human history is shaped. Each time a man stands up for an ideal, or acts to improve the lot of others, or strikes out against injustice, he sends forth a tiny ripple of hope, and crossing each other from a million different centres of energy and daring, those ripples build a current which can sweep down the mightiest walls of oppression and resistance.

Presence flows from a speaker's authenticity and focus. We all have different sides of who we are. At different times we may be serious, playful, flirtatious, intense, calm and so on. The tone or mood we display should fit with our content and the objectives we'd like to achieve with the particular speech or moment. The audience wants to see you, not your idea of what an audience might like. You are interesting enough. Never worry about whether you are compelling or interesting.

While I have been writing this book, many young students have been delivering speeches, probably for the first time in their lives, on gun violence. I was particularly struck by the stage presence of 18-year-old Emma González, a school shooting survivor who included a stretch of silence lasting six minutes and 20 seconds in the second half of her speech in Washington, DC, on 17 February 2018. This was the exact amount of time the active shooter was in her high school. Her gravitas and vulnerability, standing and breathing in this silence, brought her and her schoolmates' experience directly to the audience. The authenticity and presence of this young student were tremendous and enabled her to connect with people across political boundaries.

LISTEN

*"I would trade all my technology for
an afternoon with Socrates."*
Steve Jobs

I've defined stage presence as the ability to command attention. A fully present speaker who is in the moment and focused on what they are saying, without worrying about perfection, will always be interesting to watch. When I say 'in the moment', I mean someone who is not thinking ahead and is therefore not worried about anything other than what they are communicating at that moment.

This comes with practice. You must get out of your own way. You must work to lessen the things that hold you back psychologically and in your mindset. You must consciously cultivate the use of your instrument and regulate your physiological responses. You need to accustom yourself to a strong, confident delivery. You are grounded in your purpose, not the things you cannot control. Finally, in order to have a commanding presence, you need to learn to listen. This is, perhaps, the defining, most powerful element of a mature, effective speaker.

If you ask entrepreneurs, or those in the tech industry, who their favourite speaker is, Steve Jobs is usually at the top of their list. It could be argued that this is because of his achievements as an innovator. Yet, at the same time, there is something compelling about him. His presence captivates. I believe this is because of his pacing and ability to listen.

During his 2005 Stanford Commencement Address, when the audience laughs, Jobs pauses and smiles. His body language shows he is laughing quietly with them. During the unveiling of the iPhone at Apple, the audience is repeatedly cheering and clapping. He joins this exuberance in his own way by pacing on the stage, smiling and acknowledging the excitement. He does not try to control the crowd or hush them. Instead, he listens and responds appropriately. Even on the stage, the audience knows he's listening to them.

Previously, I compared John F. Kennedy and Robert F. Kennedy. Both were great speakers and both listened. For a very obvious and profound example of listening, look at Robert's impromptu speech the night Dr Martin Luther King Jr was shot. He went to a gathering in Indianapolis, announced the assassination, and allowed for long pauses while the audience cried out in shock, grief and anger. He acknowledged their feelings and asked for peace. He asked them to go home and pray for Dr King, his family and America. Indianapolis was one of the few major cities in the US that did not riot that night. This may not have been the case, had Robert not gone there to speak and listen.

DISCONNECTING AND RECONNECTING

If you start disconnecting from the audience, you will be sending that message to others. If you are distracted while speaking by intrusive thoughts or an external stimulus, the audience will feel it. They may listen to you, and possibly like you and what you have to say, but they will not be captivated. If you are working on leadership, this area is particularly important, as you need to gain the trust of your audience in order to lead them.

If you do get distracted, don't deny it. Acknowledge it (to yourself) and consciously bring your attention back to the room, the people in the room, your message and so forth. This is not just about your being present. It's about creating conditions for others to be present. Speak to the entire room and listen to the whole room.

Technically speaking, when the audience laughs, boos or applauds, you'll need to pause. Trying to speak over the natural reactions of your audience is rude and creates distance. Think of your speech as a conversation. You may be doing most of the talking, but you still need to listen and take in the audience.

Why is listening so powerful? Scientific studies into mirror neurons and the complex interplay of our nervous systems are exploring the physical mechanism of what is a very intuitive, immediate experience. We all react, to one degree or another, to others. If your presence is strongly self-regulating and grounded, you may be less affected by others. On the flipside, if to some degree your presence is unstable in any one moment or situation, you may be more reactive than responsive.

Our ears do not only take in sound. They are also involved in our sense of balance and our relationship with the Earth and movement. Listening also has a physical quality of spaciousness and receptivity that supports connection. When we are listening well, even if we are speaking, we are communicating and entraining respect for and connection with the audience. The message we are giving is for that audience. Active listening – acknowledging that we have heard another by saying back to them in our own words what we've heard – brings us into a deeper relationship with whoever we are with.

These are skills and habits we can learn and progress in. The more we practise and bring these qualities to our awareness and interactions, the more they will become second nature.

PRESENCE IN INTERVIEWS, MEETINGS AND LEADERSHIP

"Knowledge speaks, wisdom listens."
Jimi Hendrix

A listening presence is crucial in job interviews. The interviewer is asking questions because they want to know what your answer is. Yet, too many times in interviews the interviewee will be so focused on the outcome of the interview that they have a hard time staying in the moment and listening. When this happens, it is hard to give clear, concise answers. See the exercises at the end of this chapter to set yourself up for a successful interview.

Take a moment to think about a time when you felt really heard in a meeting. Perhaps you were speaking to your colleagues or your boss, and they were listening carefully and interested in what you were saying. How did you feel? When I am speaking and the listener is trying to interrupt, my body tenses. However, when the listener is taking in what I am saying and it's clear they are listening to understand and not to interrupt, my body is relaxed and I feel heard and validated.

If you are in a position of leadership and carry an undercurrent of hostility or a lack patience, your team members are not likely to feel supported when they speak. This means they will hold back ideas and opinions. My advice is to ask these questions:

- How do I come across in meetings?
- Does my team feel they can talk to me?
- Do I have an approachable presence in meetings?

If you don't know the answers, ask your team. They will tell you. Your job is to listen.

If employees feel listened to, if they are seen and heard, if their thoughts are considered in planning and decision-making, they are often more motivated. Even if you do not like their ideas, the fact that you listened is a critical part of leadership that builds strong teams. It gives opportunities for constructive feedback and moving forward.

INTROVERTS AND EXTROVERTS

Introverts and extroverts often have different needs and respond differently to circumstances. Some introverts will go onto a stage or prepare to lead a meeting with a strong impulse to physically hide. The work here is to acknowledge that impulse, without acting on it, while grounding and centring yourself in your purpose for speaking, your delivery and your breathing – trust these supports.

For an extrovert, meanwhile – and this greatly depends on the person – the stage may feel very inviting. Some speakers who particularly like attention – who enjoy the process of public speaking and being seen – may need to be reeled in occasionally. If you are one of those people, watch a recording of your speech and ask whether your enjoyment of presenting is overriding your message or the rest of your delivery.

THE PRACTICE
OF PRESENCE

Presence requires purpose, authenticity and active listening. It is not just something we bring to the stage. We can bring these qualities to anything we do and any circumstances we chose.

EXERCISE 33
LISTENING ON STAGE
Duration: Depends on speech length

PURPOSE: CREATE TRUST WITH AUDIENCE

You can rehearse this with any speech. If you have willing accomplices, ask them to play the part of the audience. If you are solo, use your imagination.

Step 1: Do the breath and vocal warm-up in Part 2 Exercises 11 and 18.

Step 2: Introduce yourself (or your subject) and pause appropriately.

Step 3: Acknowledge the audience by waiting for them to finish clapping or responding appropriately at the start and during your delivery.

Outcome: The audience will feel invited into the discussion as opposed to feeling talked at or dismissed. You will come across as confident.

EXERCISE 34
HOW TO PRACTICE ACTIVE LISTENING IN MEETINGS
Duration: Depends on meeting length

PURPOSE: CREATE TRUST WITH COLLEAGUES

Step 1: Slow down and slightly deepen your breathing.

Step 2: Remind yourself of your intention to listen in order to understand, and not to interrupt or push your agenda.

Step 3: Make eye contact with the speaker(s). Let them know you are listening with non-verbal communication.

Step 4: When you do speak, acknowledge another person's idea directly before or during your comments. Stay calm, clear and direct with your comments.

Outcome: You will be perceived as wise, smart and trustworthy, having listened to your team without being carried away by your need to dominate conversation or to prove your worth.

EXERCISE 35
LISTENING DURING JOB INTERVIEWS
Duration: Entire interview

PURPOSE: RESPECT INTERVIEWER
AND CREATE RAPPORT

PREPARATION FOR THE INTERVIEW

Step 1: Write a list of questions you will likely be asked, and answer them. Record yourself and then listen to the recording without criticism. Listen to see whether you are answering the question clearly and concisely.

Step 2: Write a list of goals for the interview. Make sure your goals are achievable.

THE INTERVIEW

Step 3: Do the breath and vocal capacity warm-up in Exercise 11 and 18 to ground yourself for the interview.

Step 4: Listen to the questions you are asked. If you are unclear whether you answered the question at hand, ask. For example: "Does that make sense?" or "Is that along the lines of what you were asking?"

Outcome: Listening well in interviews helps the interviewer relax and provides the opportunity for a sincere conversation. This will create a lasting impression.

DAILY LIFE

Everything I've discussed in this book can support a greater presence in your daily life. In particular, observe how others actively listen during their interactions. Beyond professionals who draw on this skill, you will find this listening quality to be relevant in many situations, as it's a very human thing to do when we are interested in another person or what they have to say.

Active listening is also a very accessible practice to bring into your own interactions. It can be direct and formal, or more casual as you find ways to acknowledge that you understood what another person said.

As you practise, what do you notice? How do conversations change? What is the impact on your experience and on your relationships? As the skill and habit take hold, you may find that you are more comfortable in silences and more present, even when the attention is not on you at all.

13.
Summary

Bringing It All Together:
A Delivery Checklist

The journey of a speaker is an ever-evolving process. My last piece of advice is to embrace this process – to enjoy the stage you're in, and work to make yourself a speaker you can step back and admire. Know that this phase will evolve into something that is perhaps deeper, richer and more thoughtful with time and attention.

Humans are not meant to be fixed creatures. When we stop growing, exploring and learning, we become deadened and bored. This is a way of cheating yourself out of life's possibilities. In the beginning of your training, fixating on an end goal with your public speaking skills will make you feel that the goal is constantly out of reach. Additionally, if you achieve the goal, you'll likely try to cling to it or get bored of it. Again, you'll be fixating on performance instead of allowing organic changes to occur and keeping your creative side invigorated.

By applying the exercises in all three parts of this book, you will always be developing your skills and abilities. You will be participating in personal and professional growth.

PRESENTATION CHECKLIST

As you come into the final stretch before giving a speech, pitch or presentation, consult this simple checklist. This goes for on-camera and off-camera speeches.

- Finish your slides ideally five to seven days before your talk.
- Ground yourself in your purpose and setting.
- Practise and time yourself.
- Ask the organizers of your talk appropriate questions so you are well prepared. For example, how large is the audience? Will I have time to do a run-through? Is there a podium?

- Wear comfortable, stylish clothes that you feel confident in.
- Avoid wearing shoes that make noise when you walk.
- Minimize the amount of jewellery that sparkles. Jewellery under lights can be distracting.

VOCAL HEALTH

As you prepare for your speech, here is my advice on keeping your voice healthy in advance:

- Reduce your consumption of coffee, orange juice and alcohol, which dehydrate the vocal folds.
- Increase your consumption of water and coconut water, which hydrate the vocal folds.
- Use your breath to fuel your voice when speaking.
- Loss of resonance, due to a virus or strain, can be helped by sipping a mixture of warm water, honey and lemon. If you've lost your voice, try not to speak unless you have to. Rest your voice.
- Use the breath and resonance exercises in Chapters 6 and 7 to keep your voice in shape.

Good luck with your journey towards becoming a confident and powerful speaker.

ACKNOWLEDGMENTS

First and foremost, thank you to Sara Taheri and the talented team at LID Publishing. The rest of my thank yous are in alphabetical order. Ann Badillo for her encouragement to start the writing process. Literary consultant, Peter Beren for sharing his amazing insight which helped me articulate what I was offering. Christine Berg for her friendship and willingness to give feedback on the exercises I developed in Part One. Consultant, Jane Freidman for sharing with me her step-by-step process for book proposals. Fay Putnam who helped me make the Alexander Technique a bit more accessible. Adam Simpson for his encouragement and good taste. Kathleen Antonia Tarr for expert legal advice. Pamela and Noel Warner, whose high standards inspired me to work harder and keep my spirits up in the face of obstacles. Nataly Michelle Wright for her early stage editing skills, support and encouragement. And finally thank you to the most beautiful, supportive and talented man I've ever known, Scott Warner.

ABOUT THE AUTHOR

Lisa Wentz has spent the past decade dedicating her life to helping professional and amateur public speakers overcome blocks, develop their voices and craft their delivery. Her background includes extensive study in psychology and ten years of professional acting training and live performance. She moved to London, UK, to earn a master's degree in Voice and Speech Studies at the Royal Central School of Speech and Drama. Upon returning to the US, she founded the San Francisco Voice Center in 2008 and has since coached public speaking clients from 37 countries.